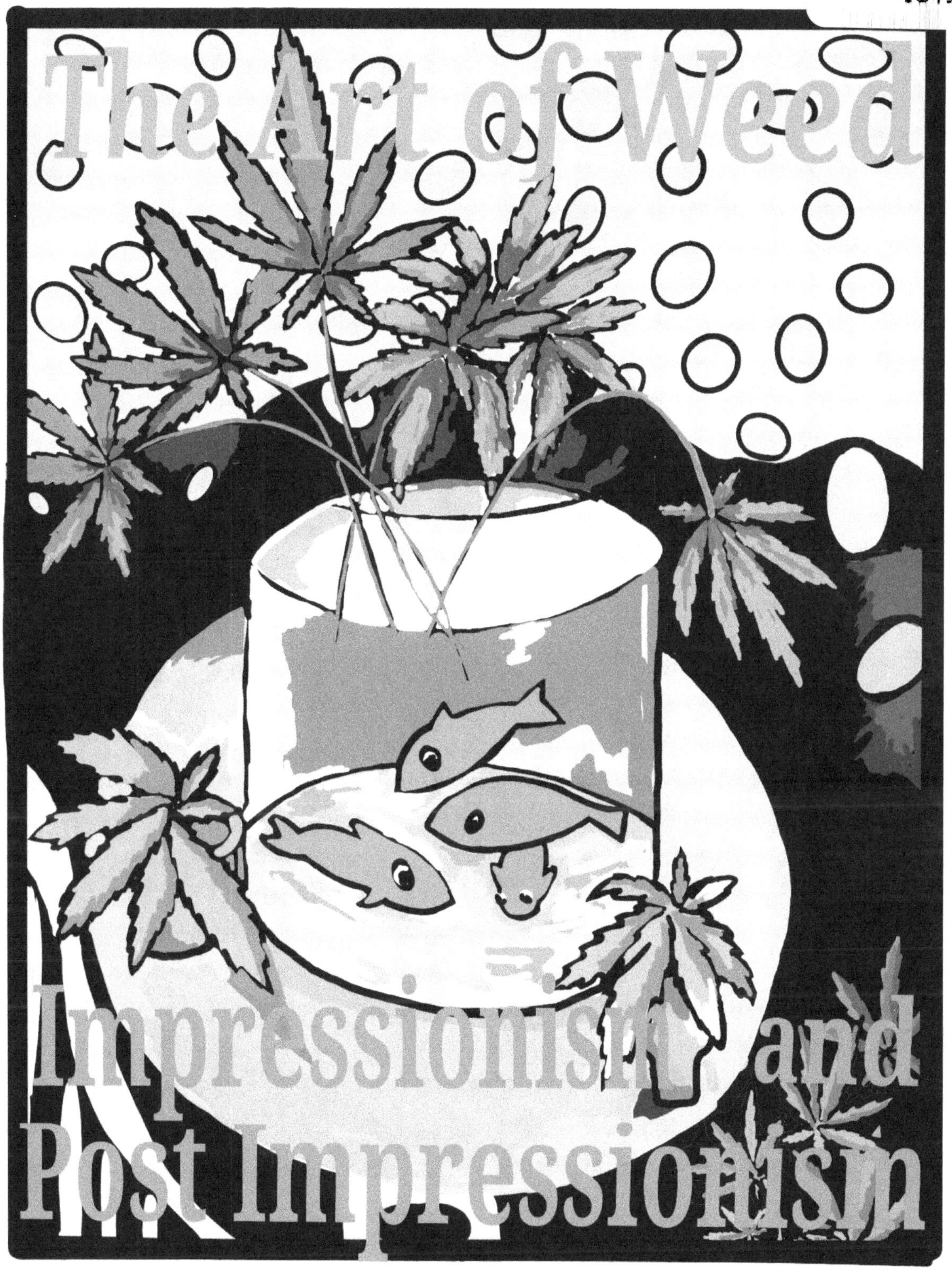

The Art of Weed

Impressionism and Post Impressionism

Copyright © 2019 Canna Mama

ISBN: 9781705952764

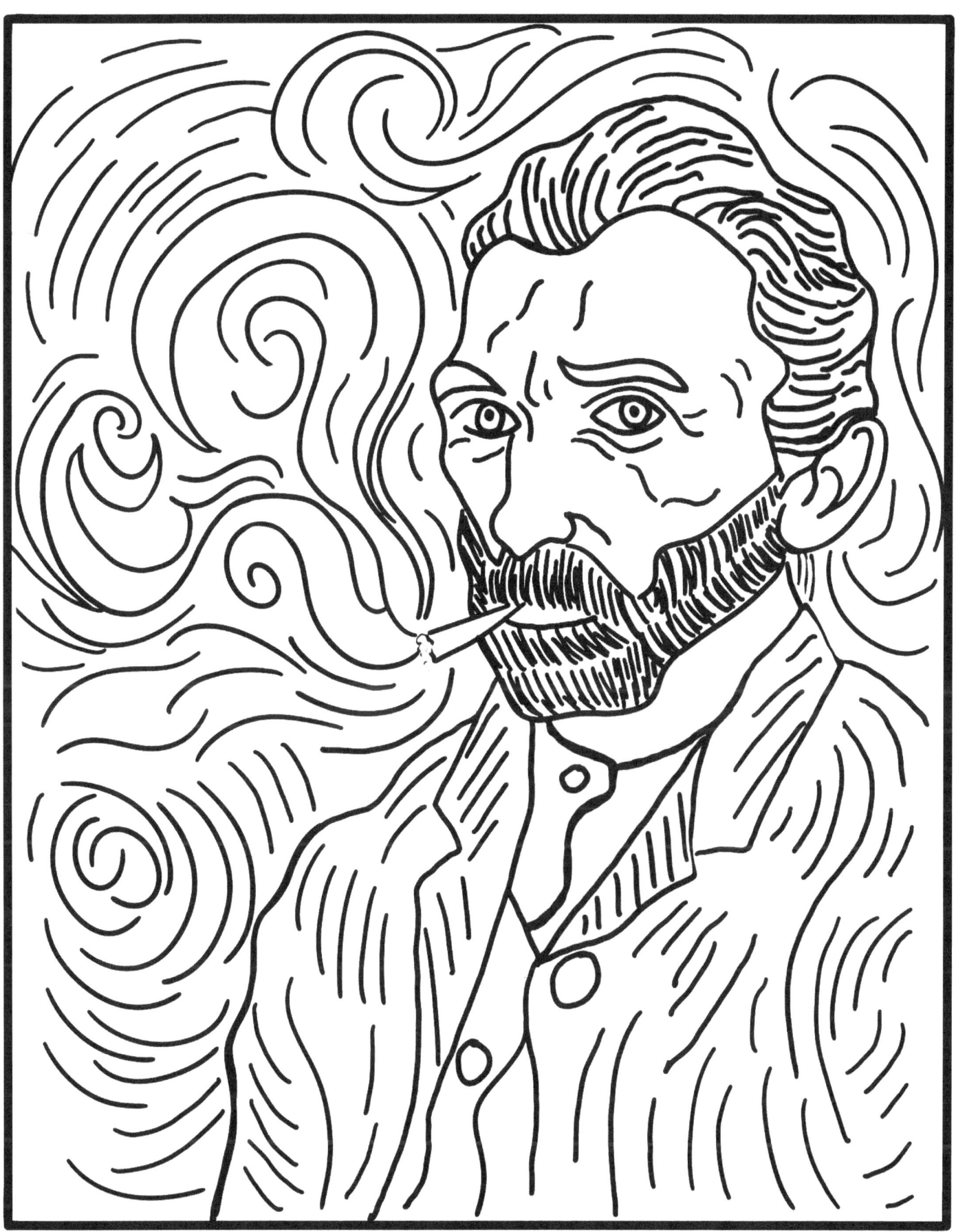

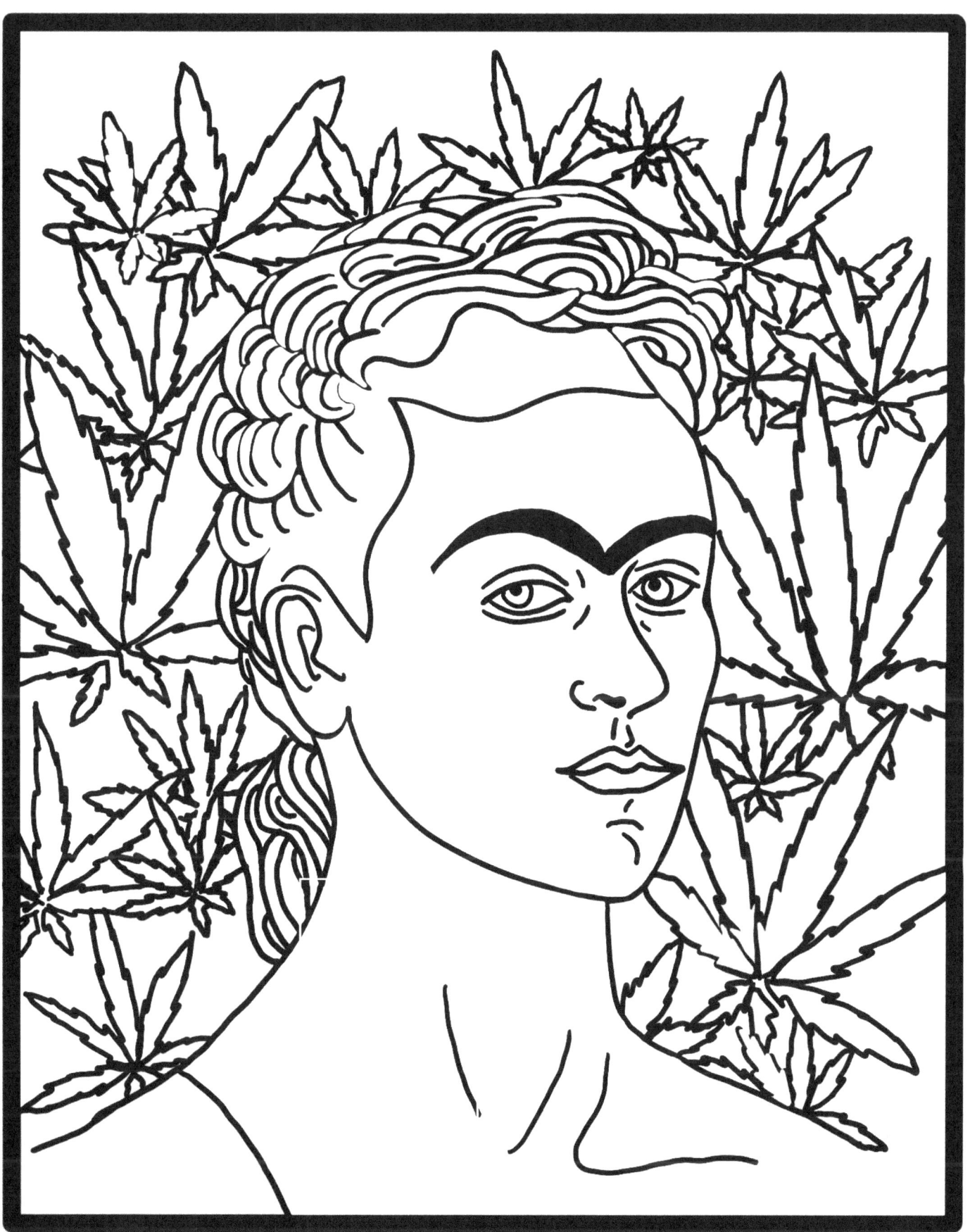

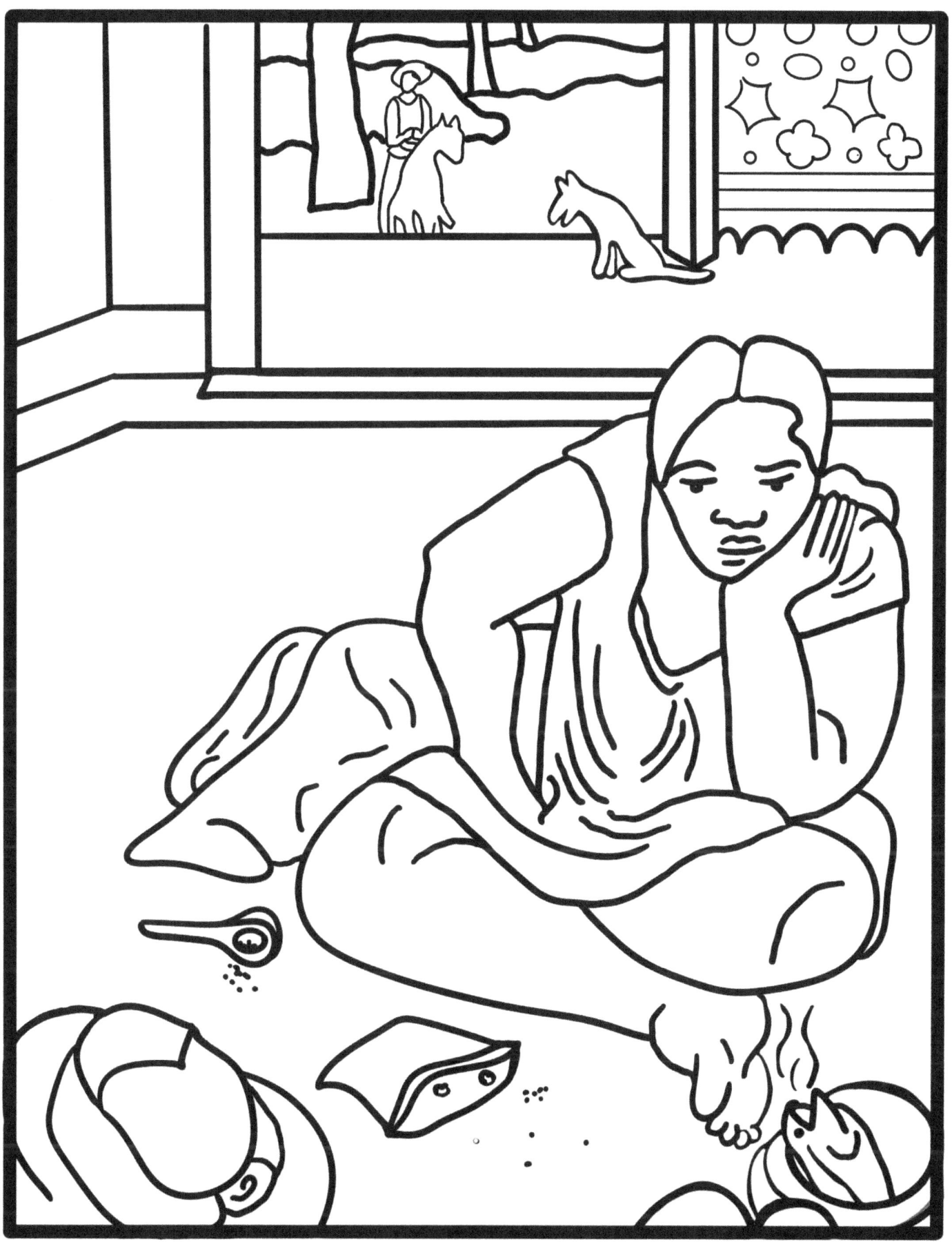

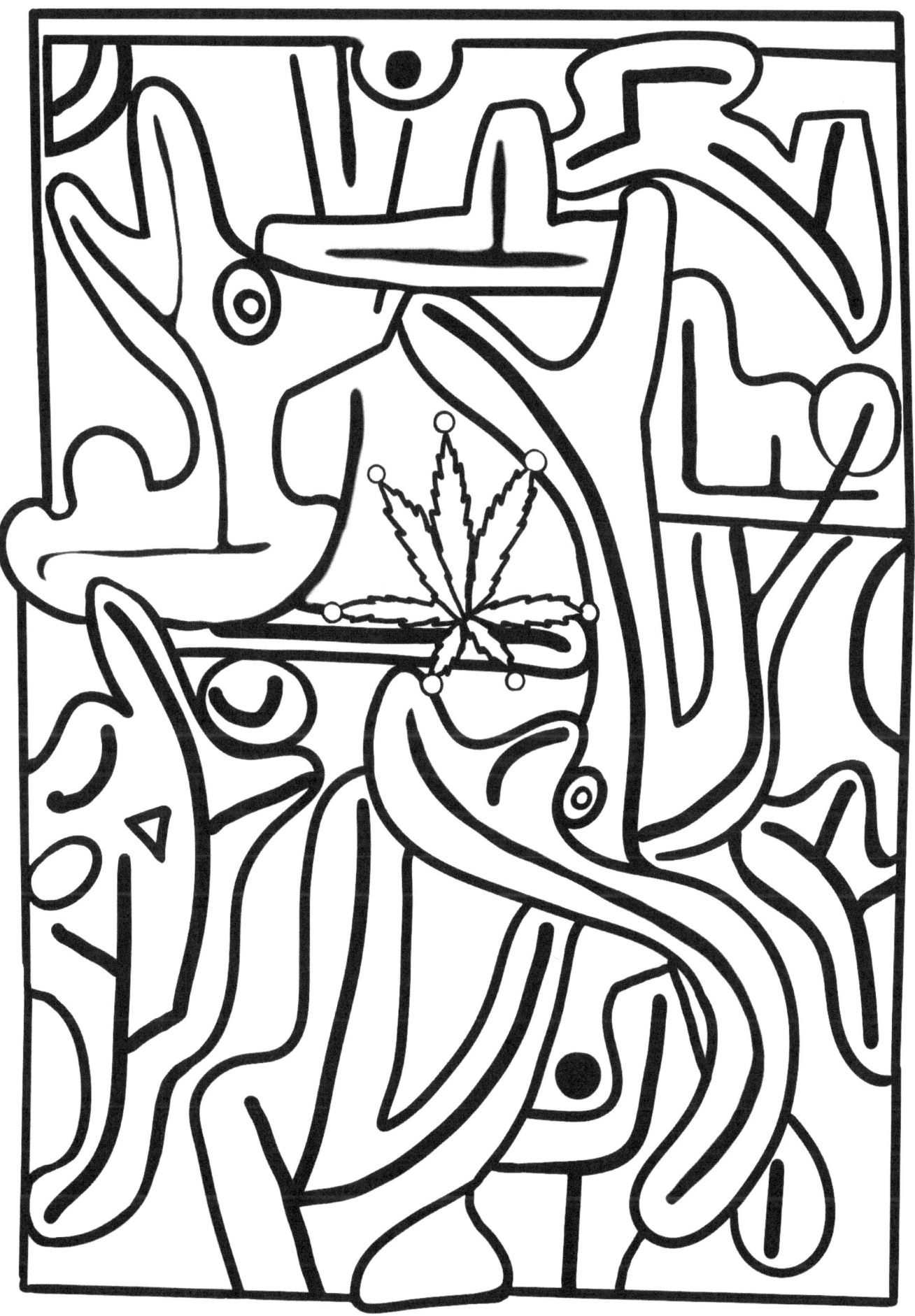

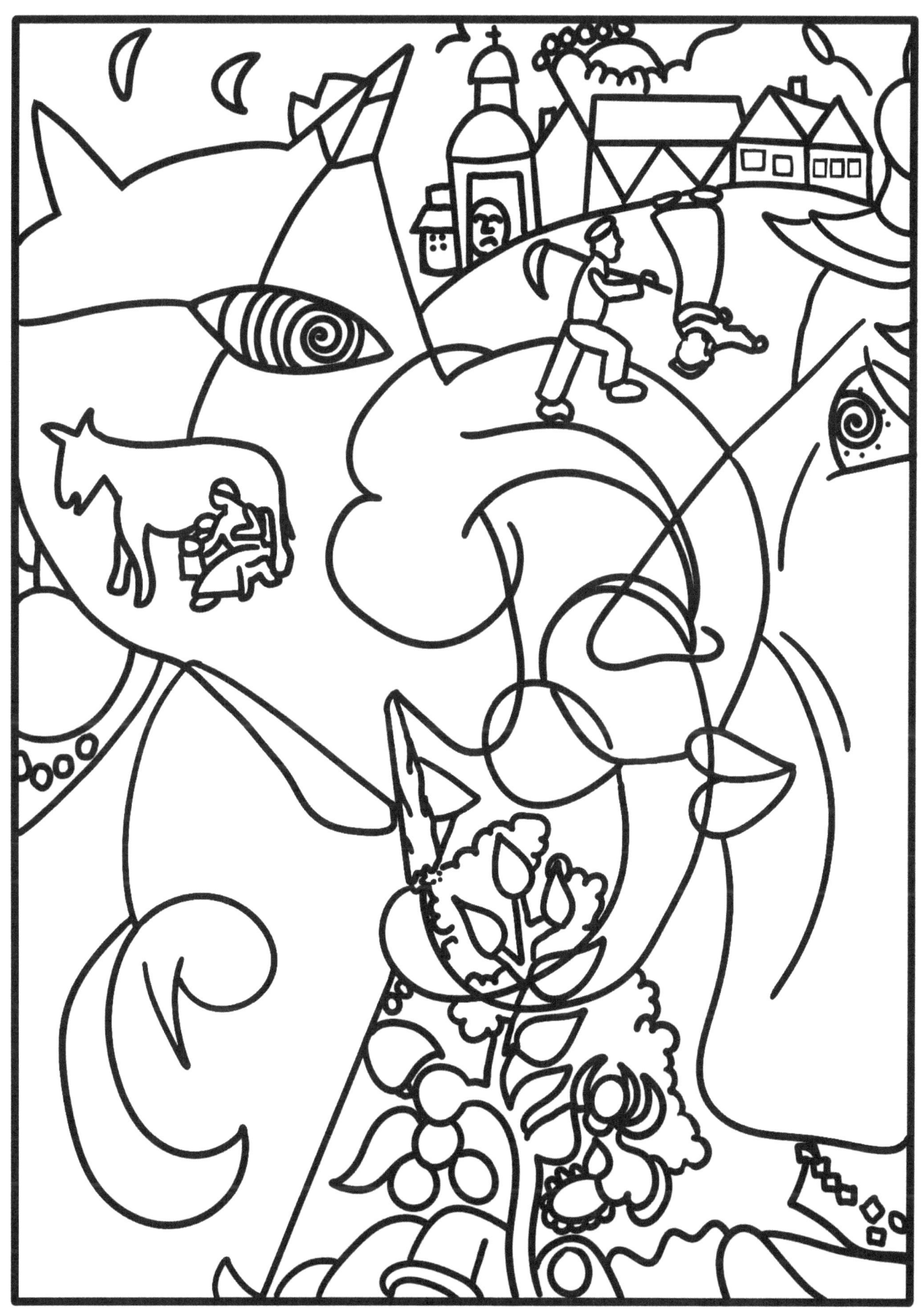

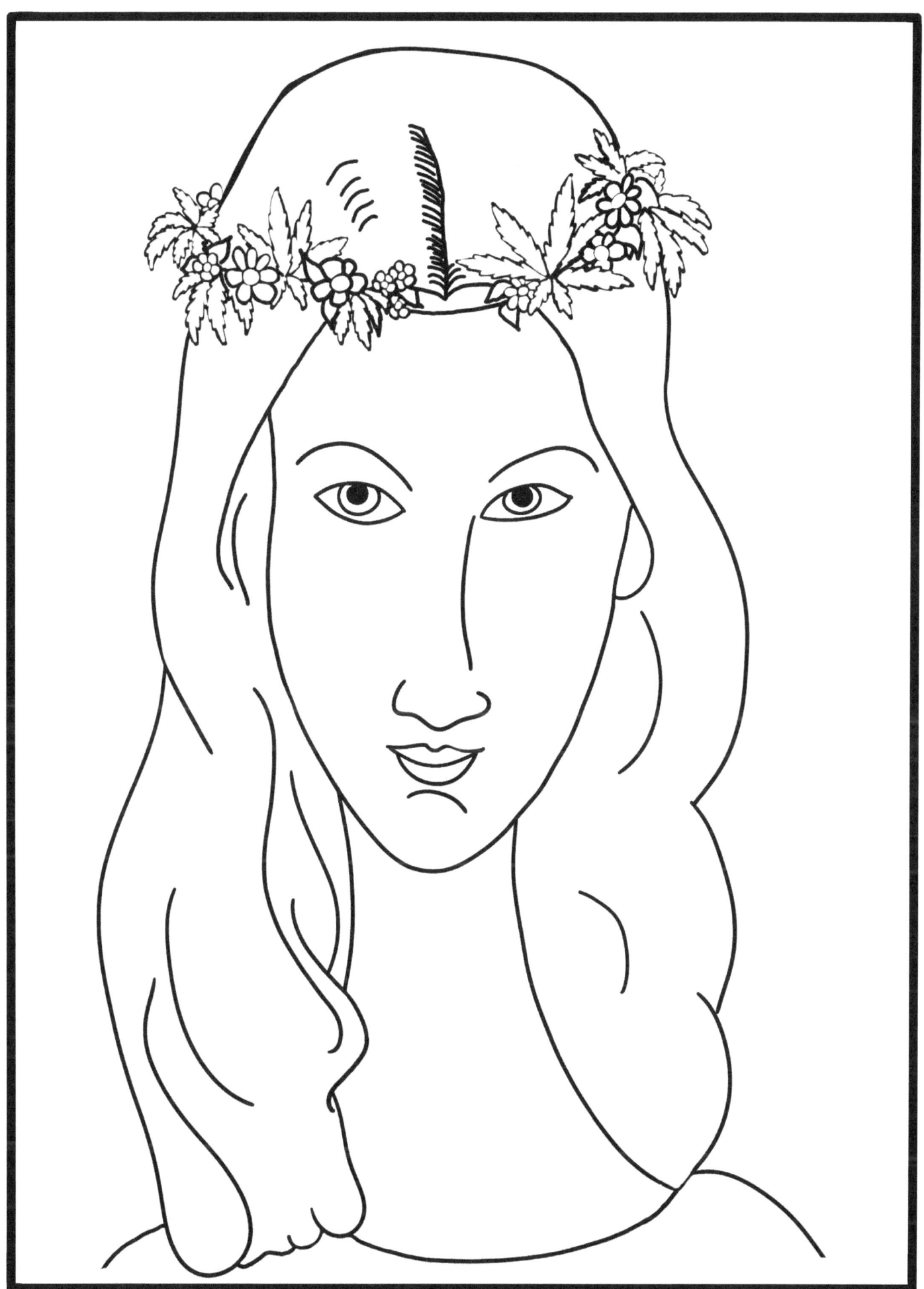

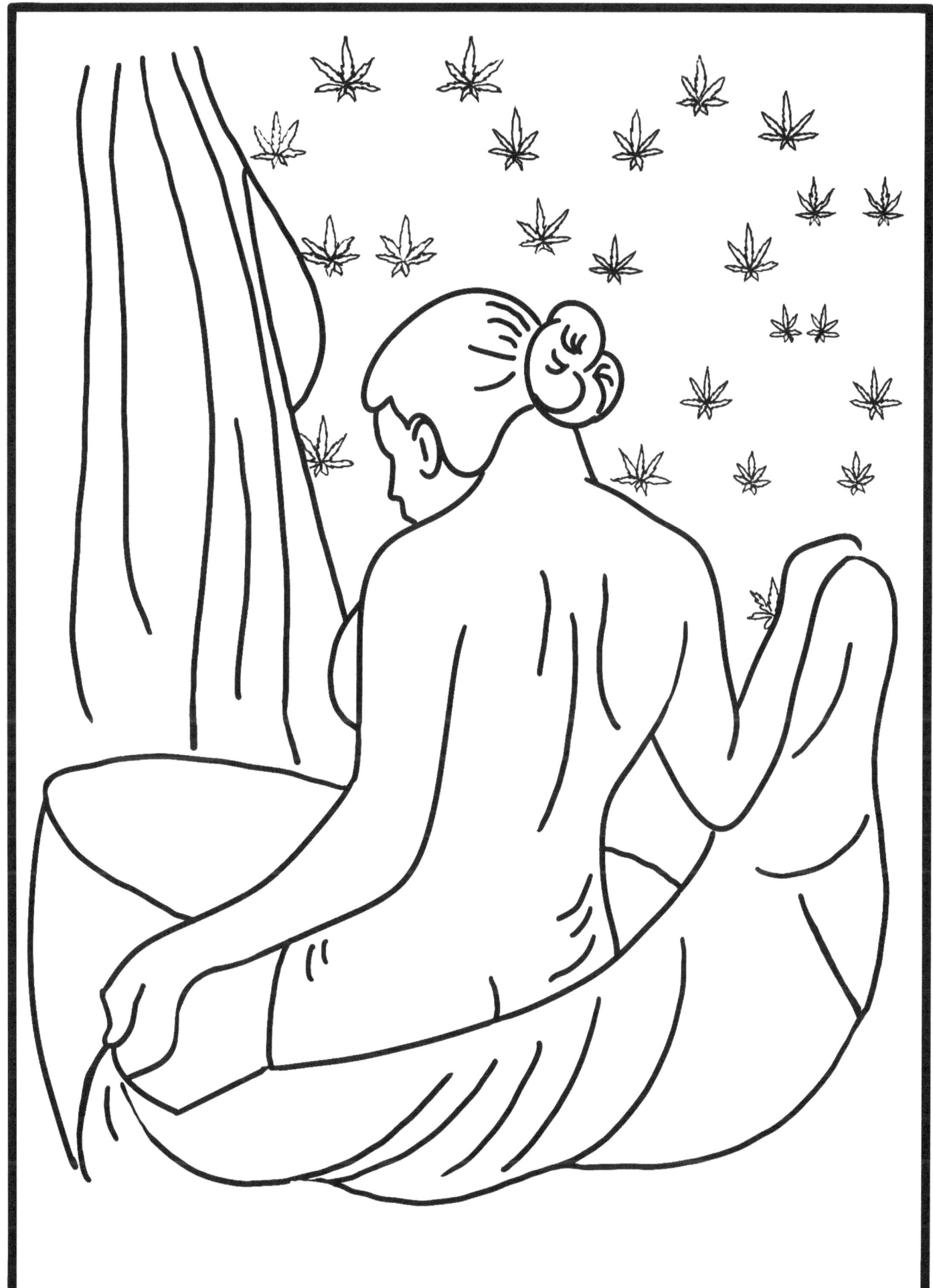

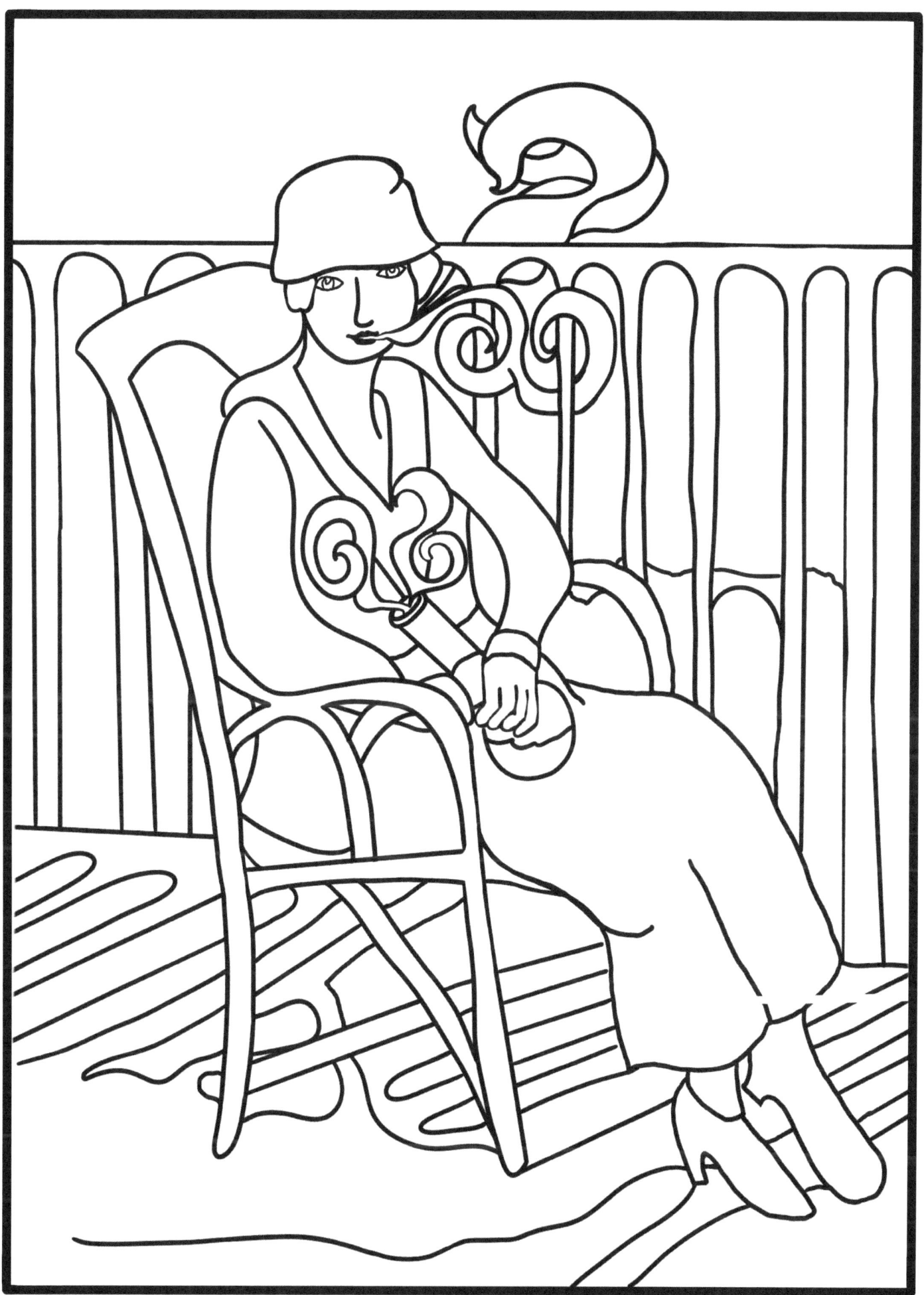

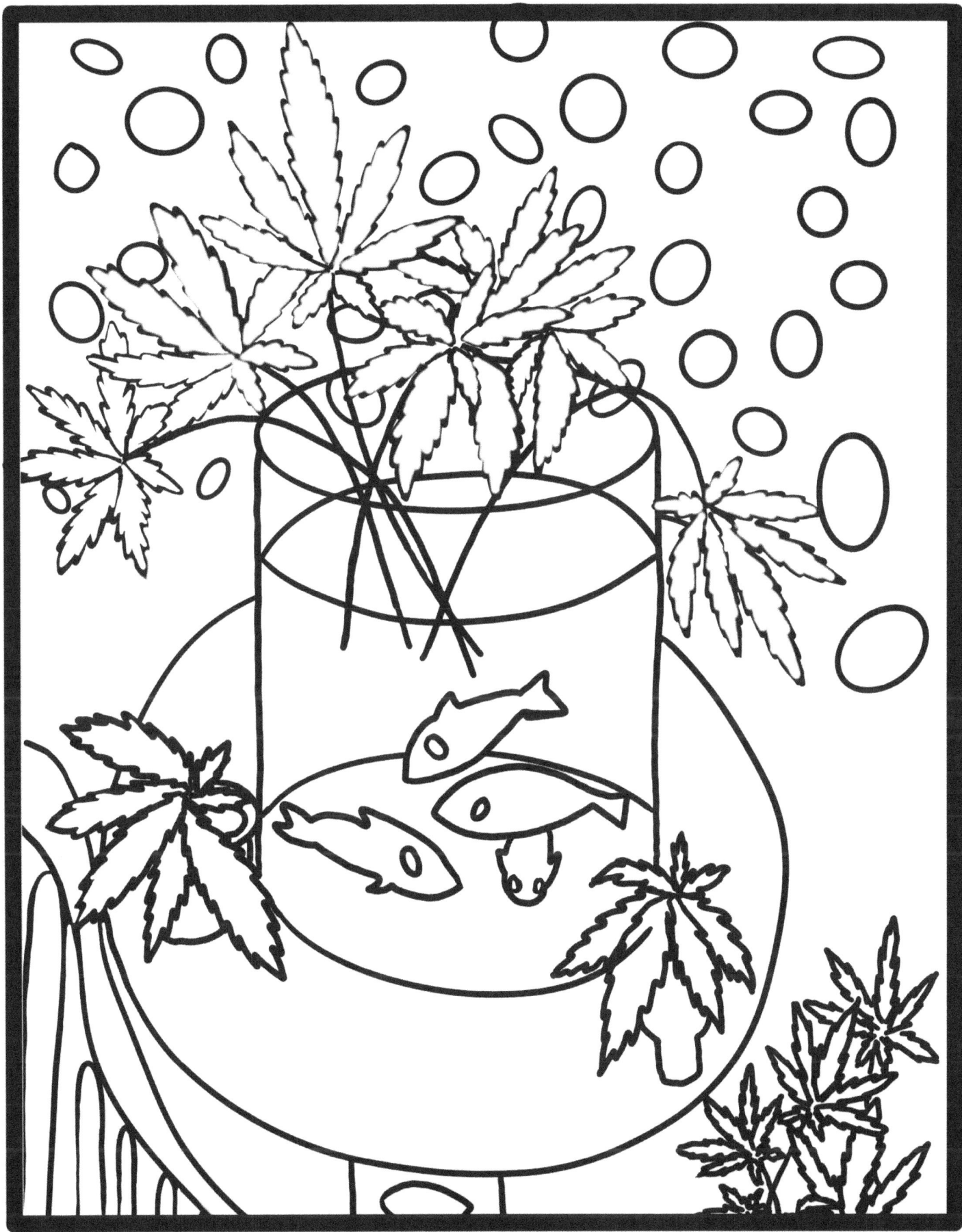

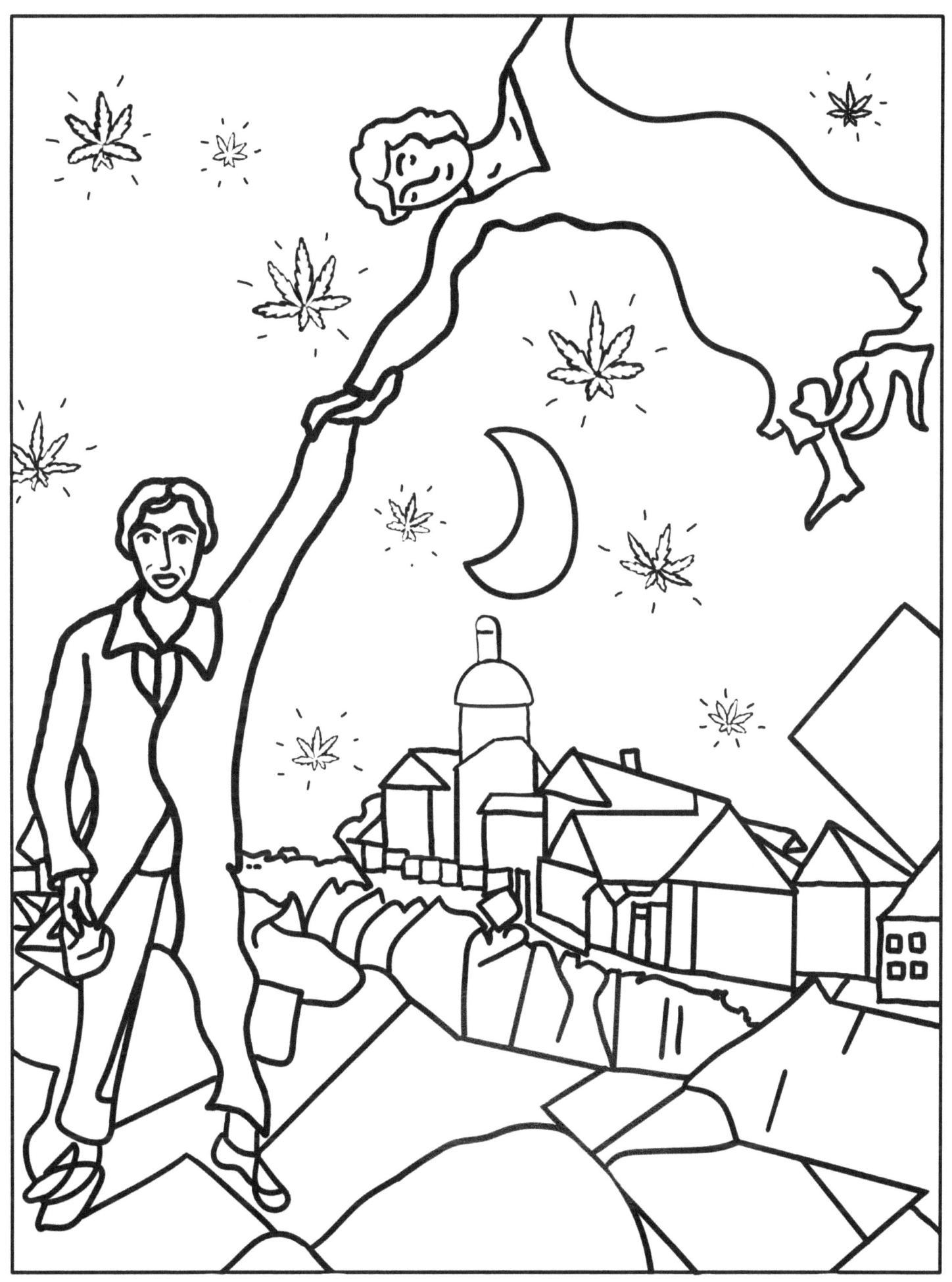

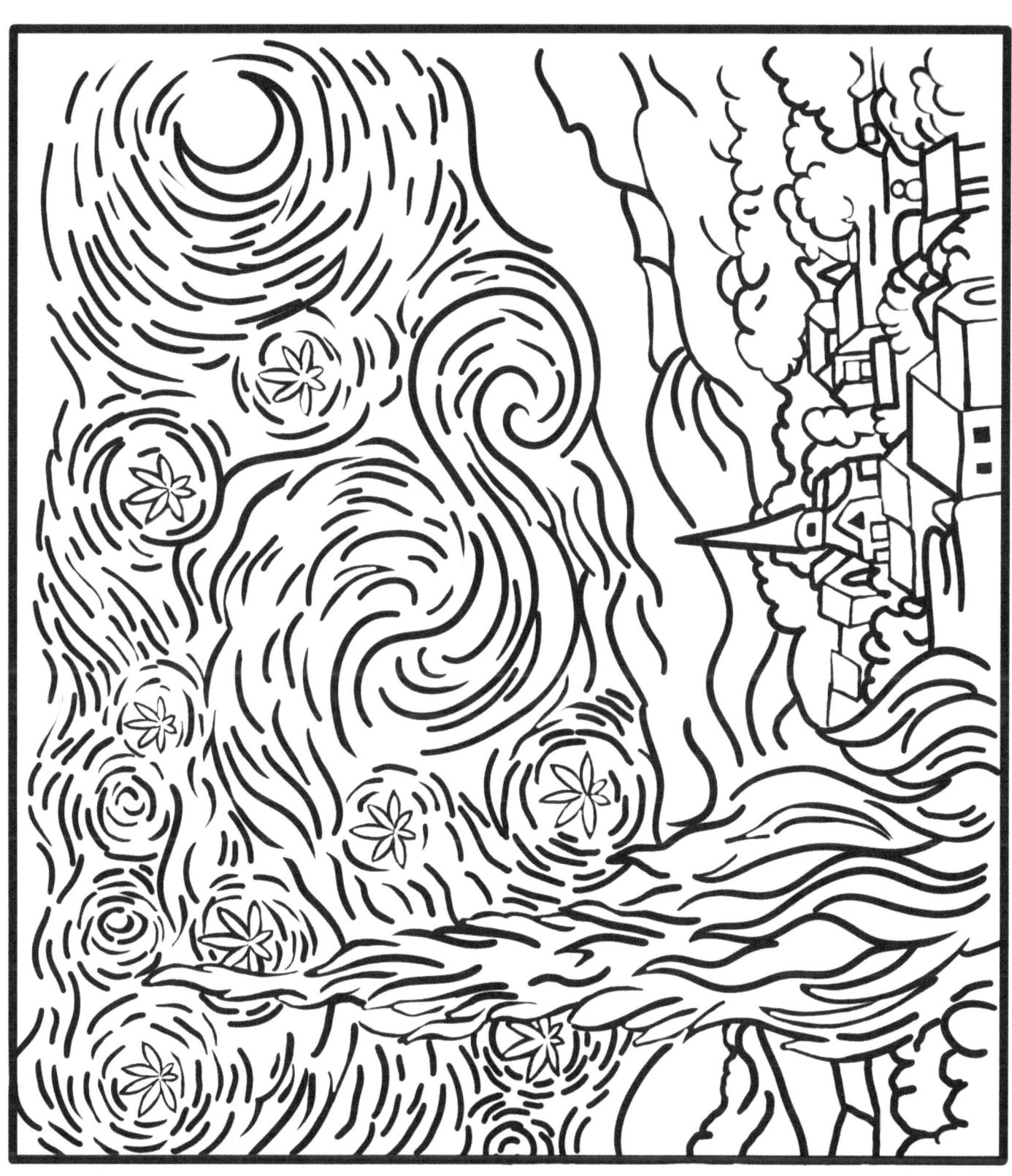

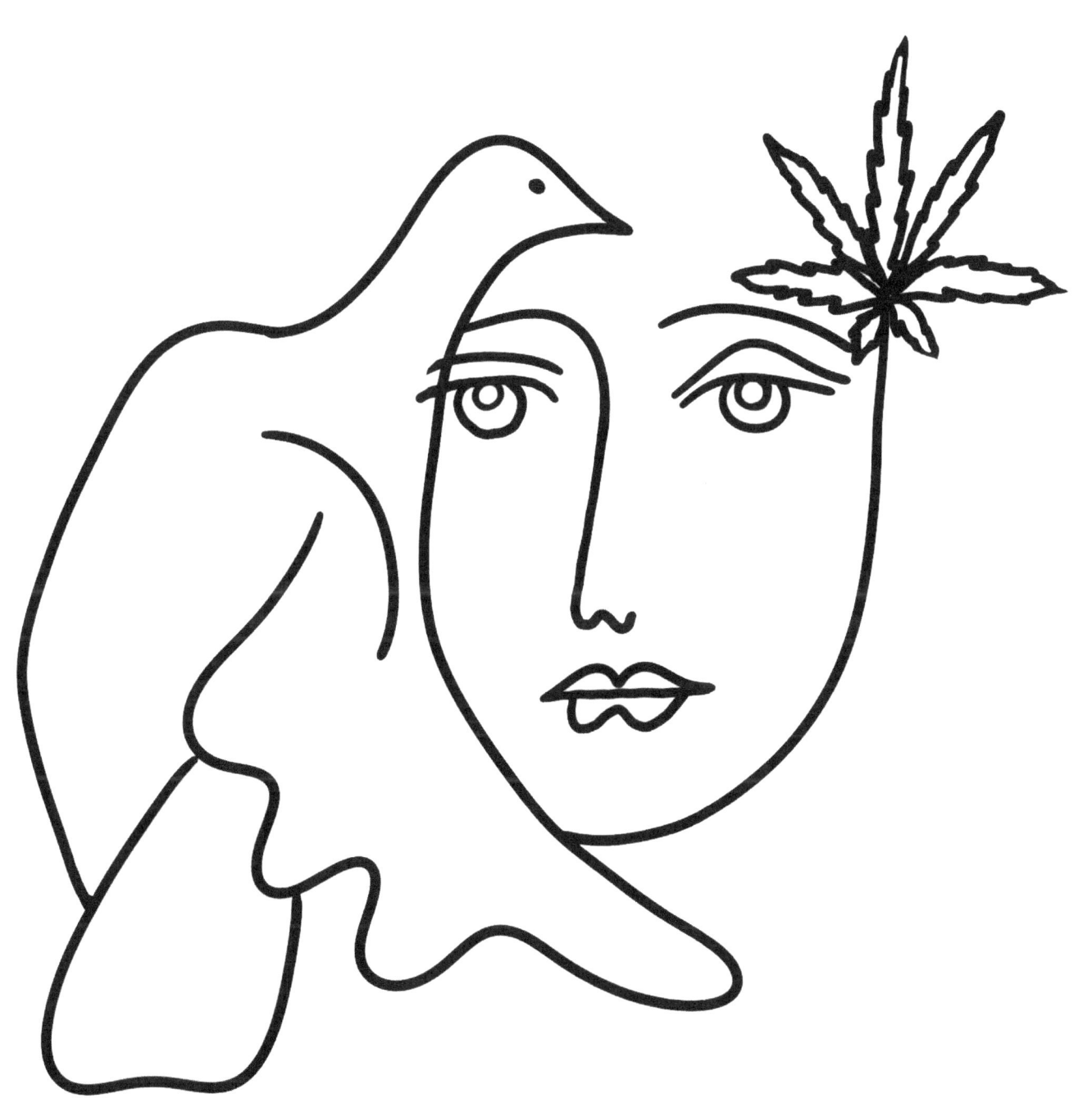

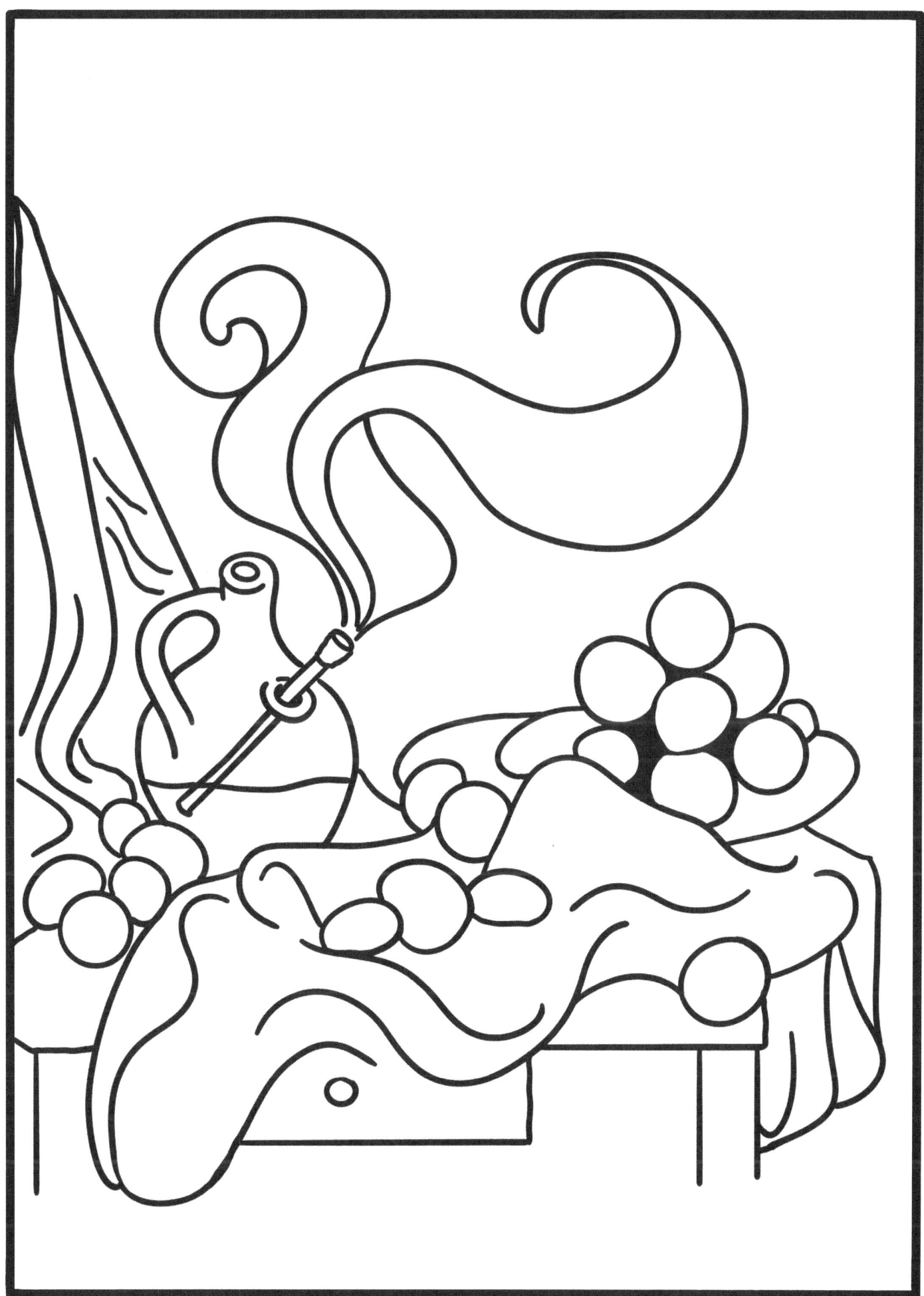

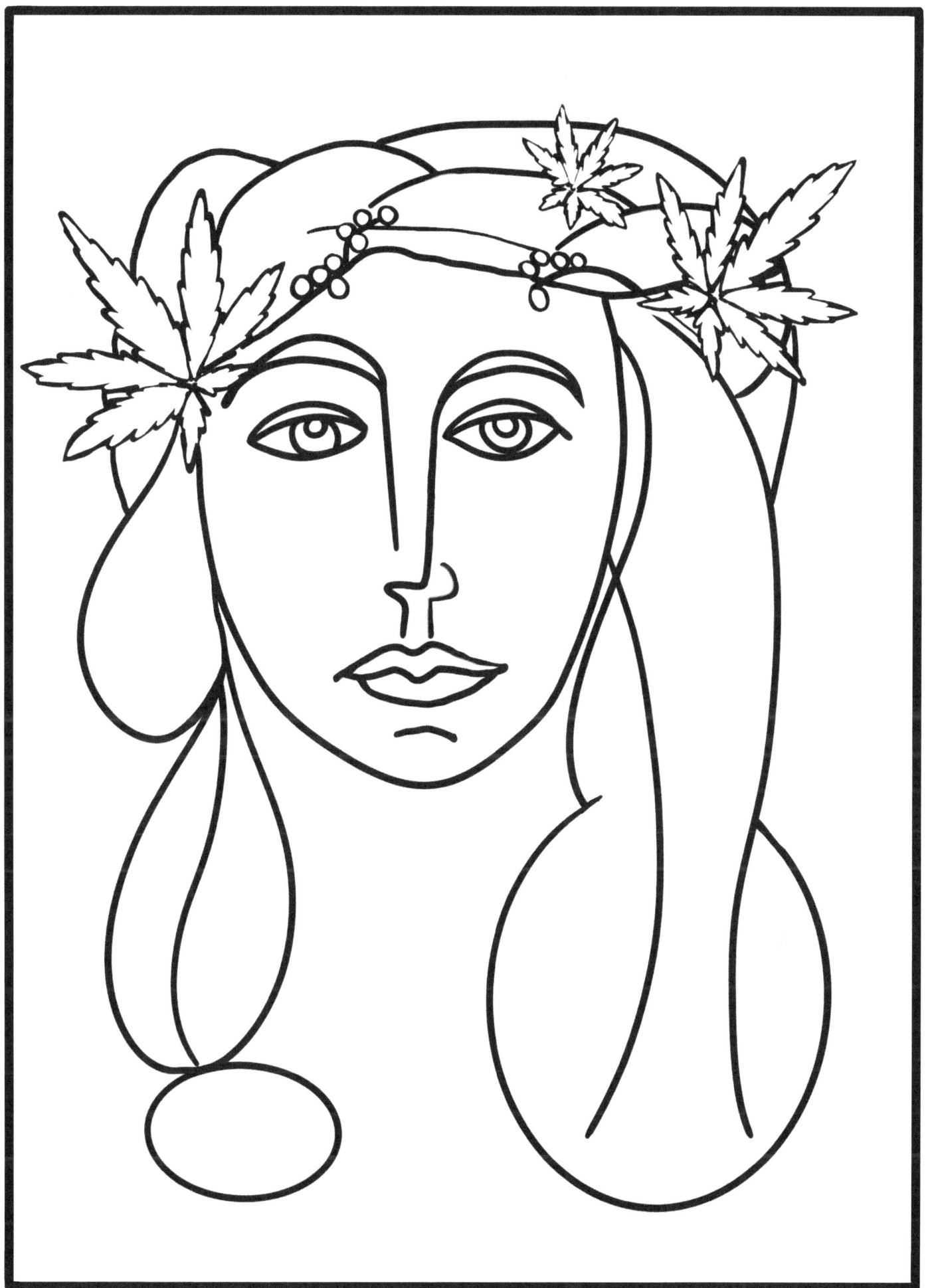

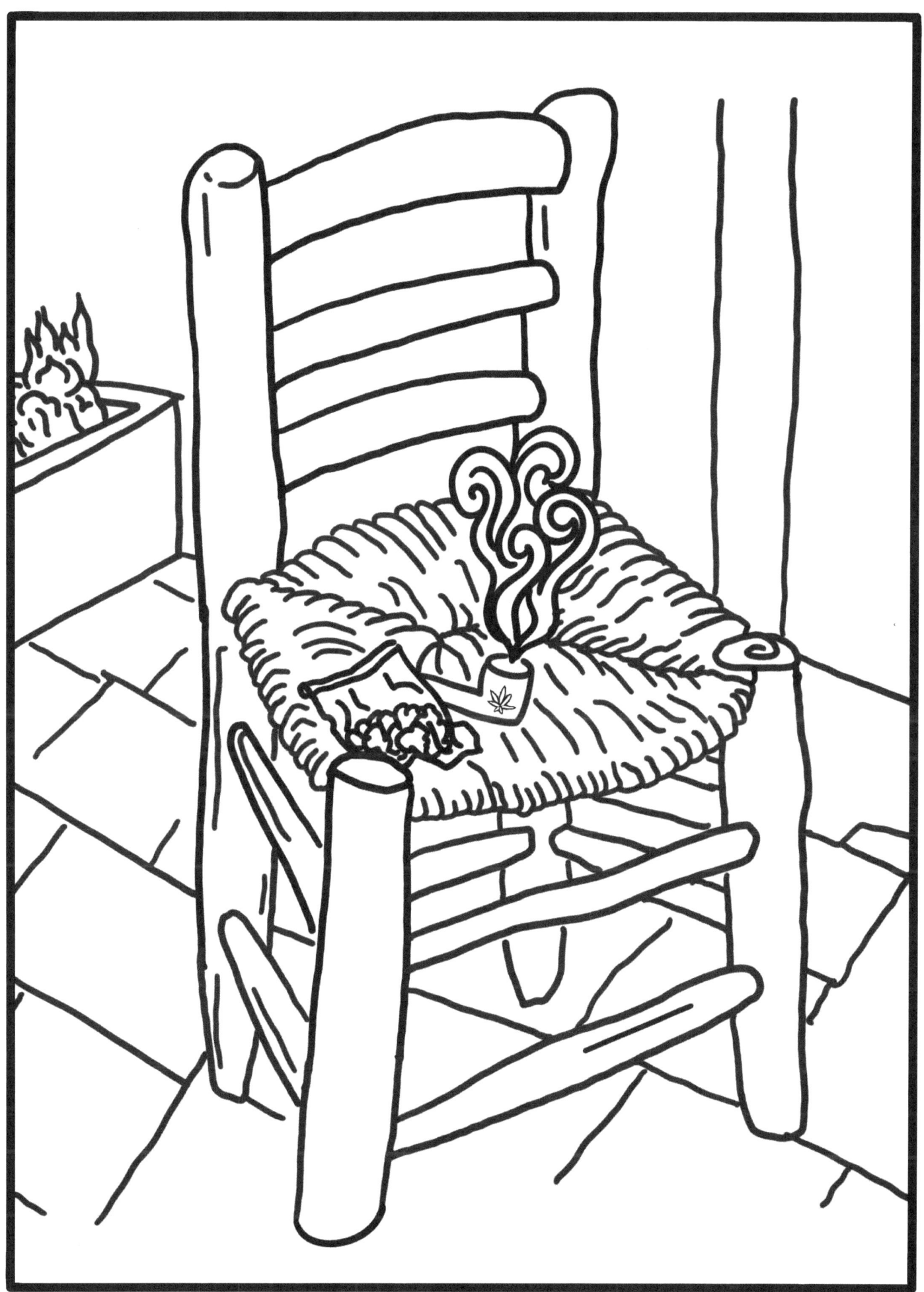

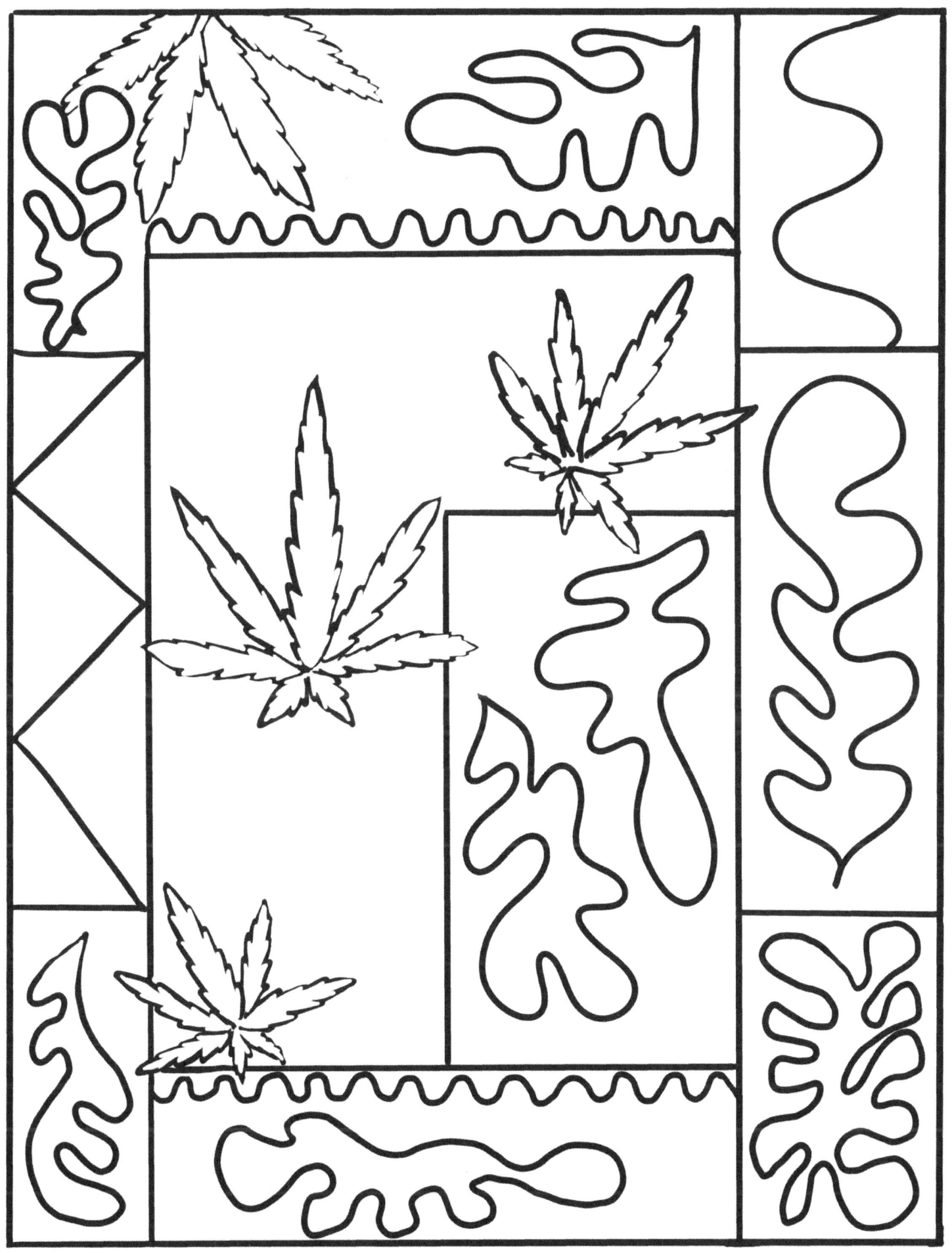

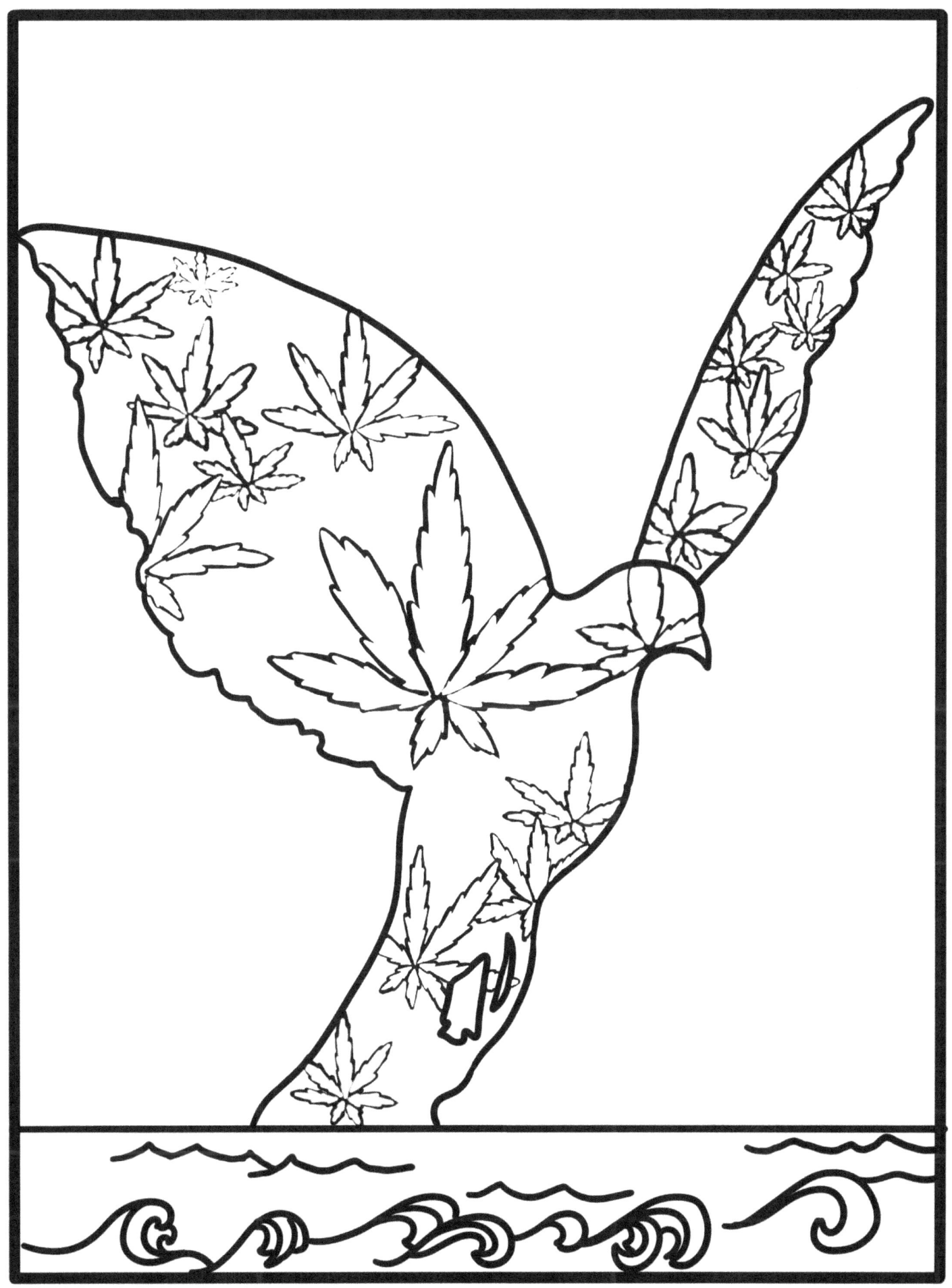

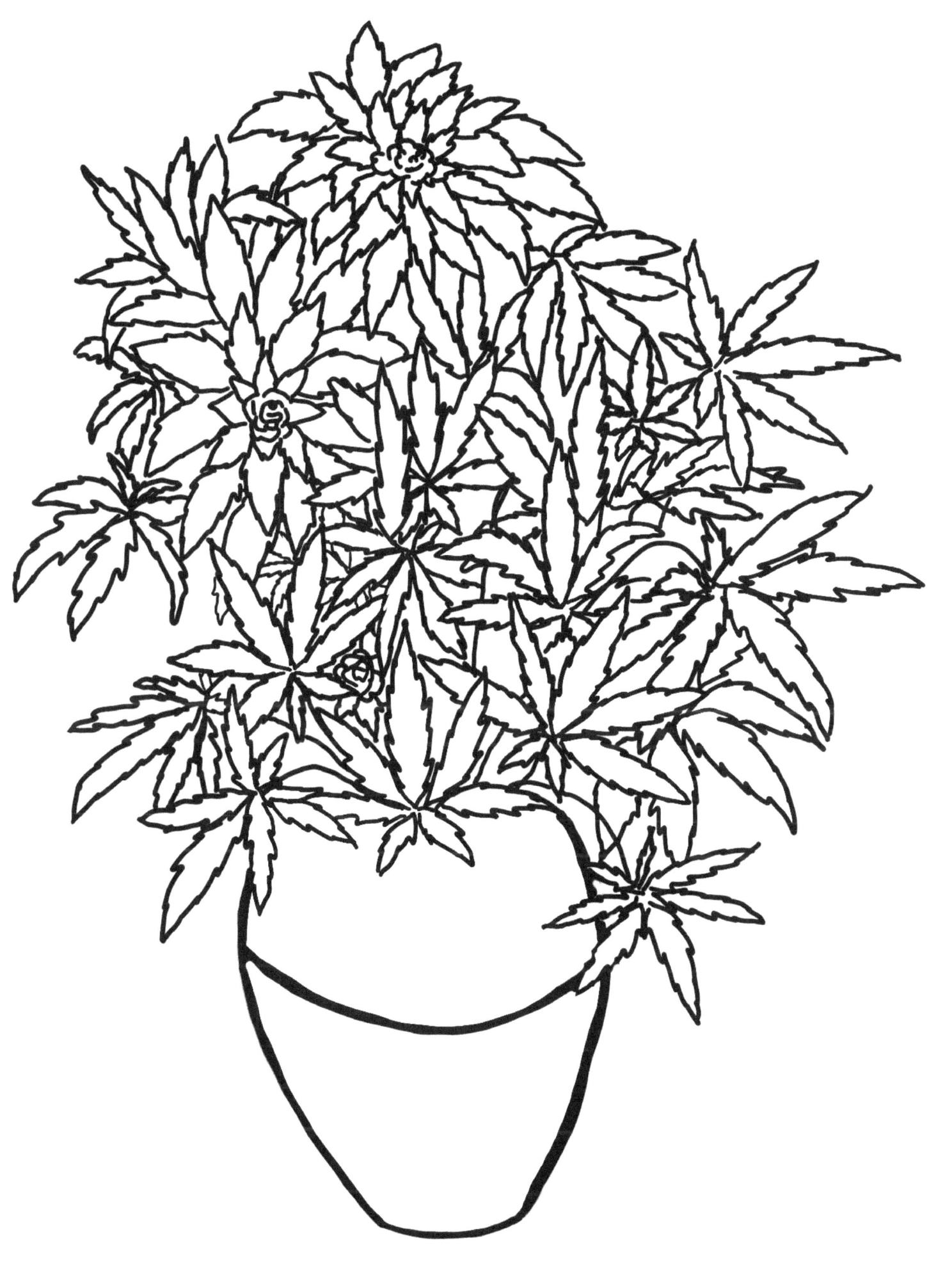

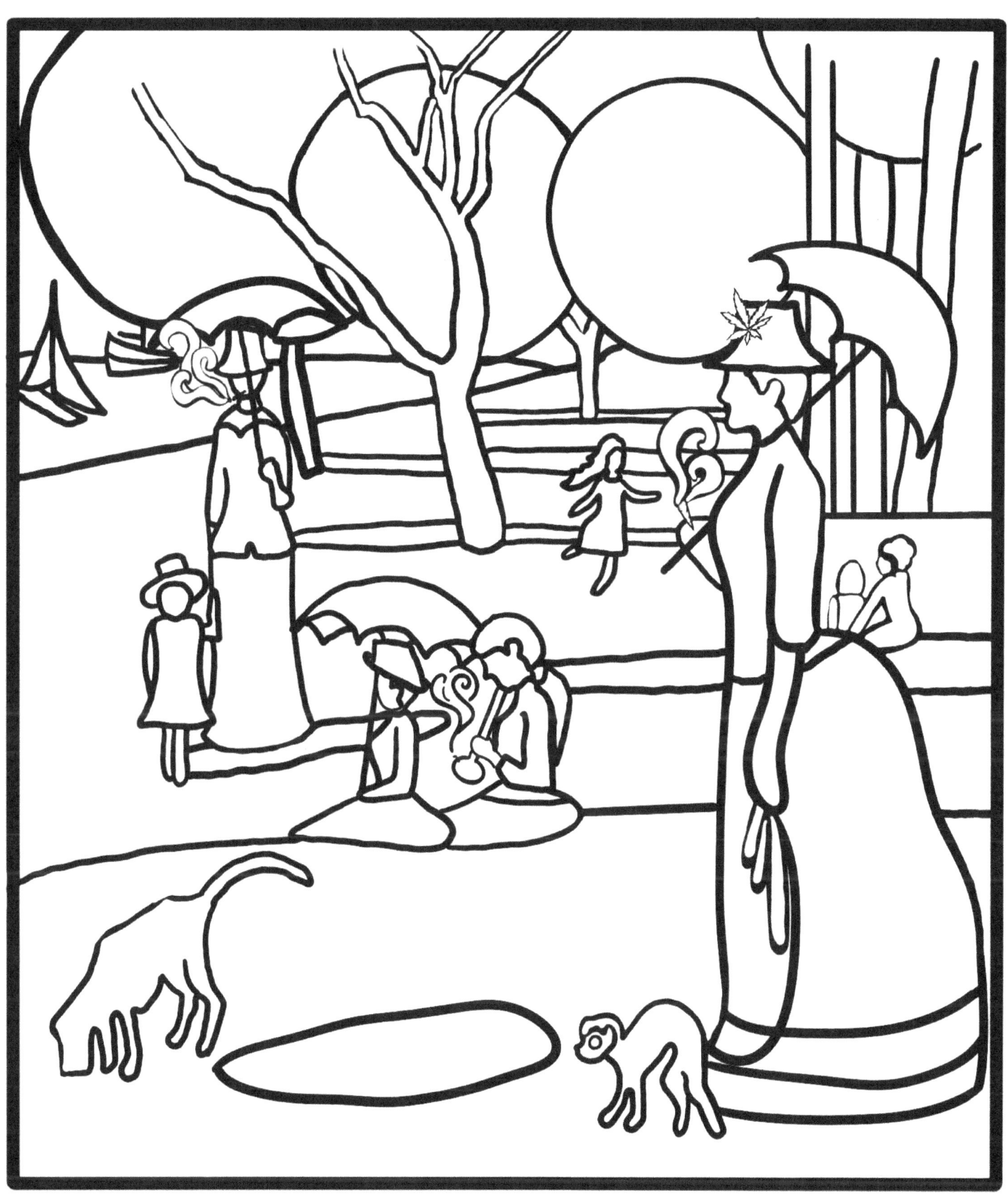

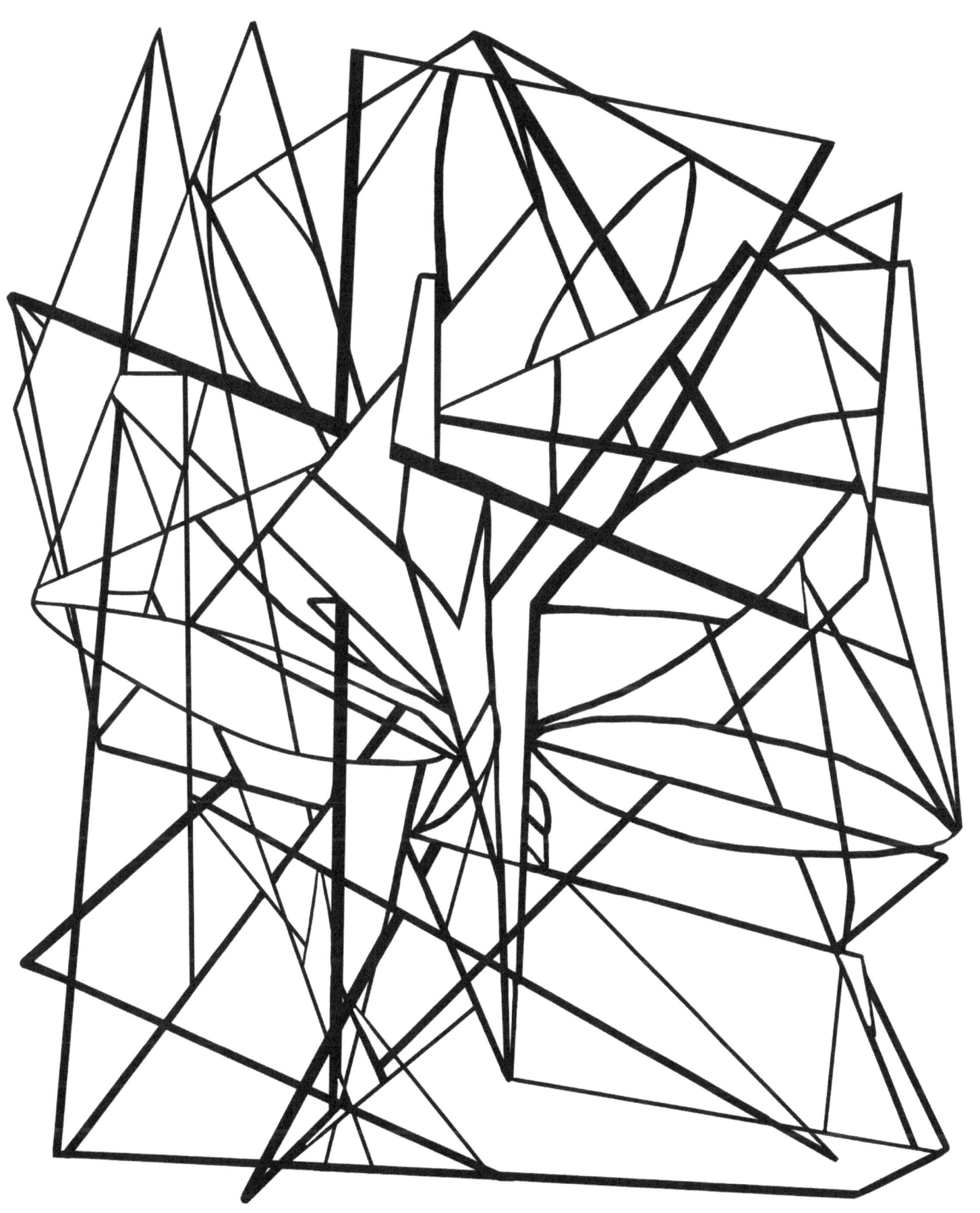

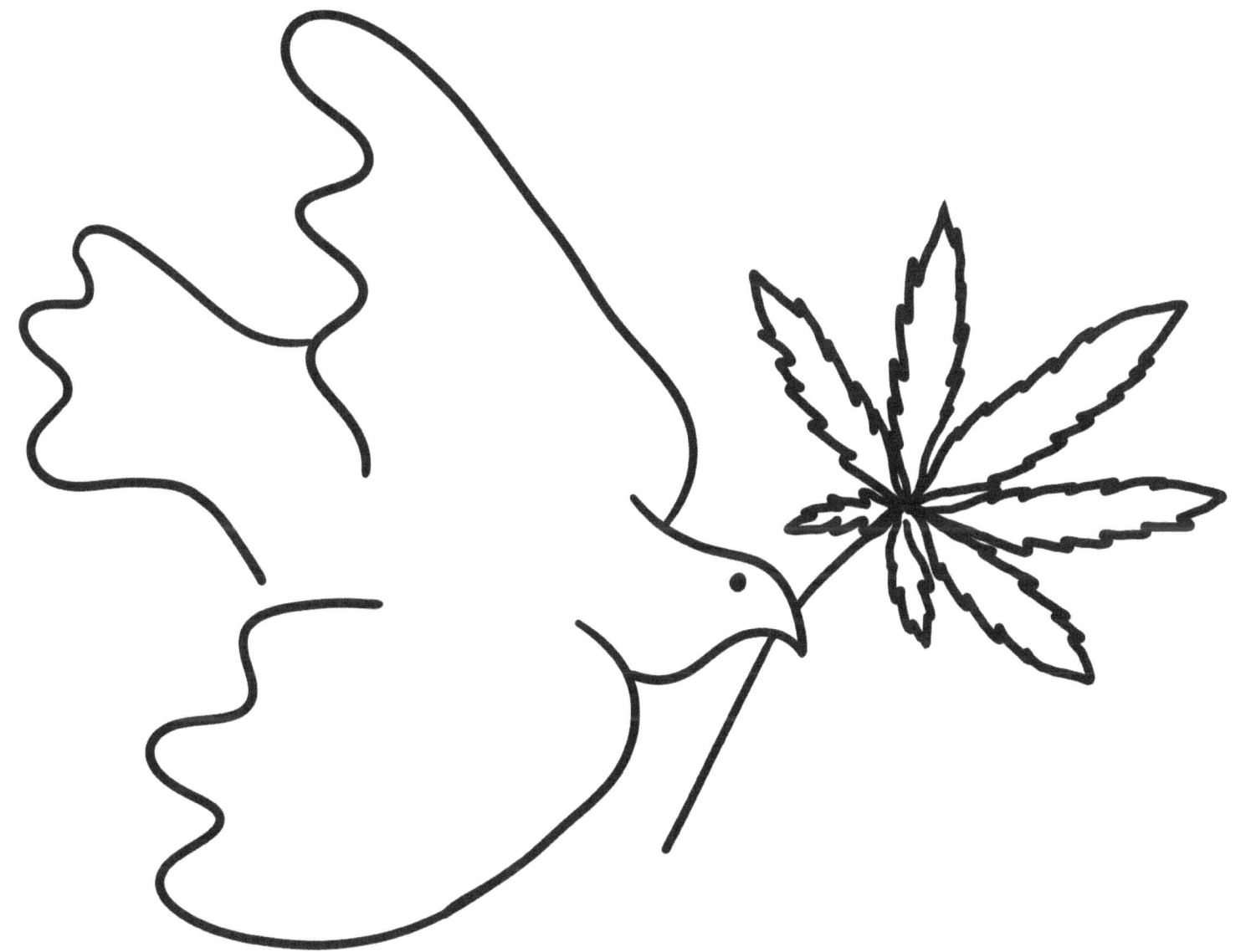

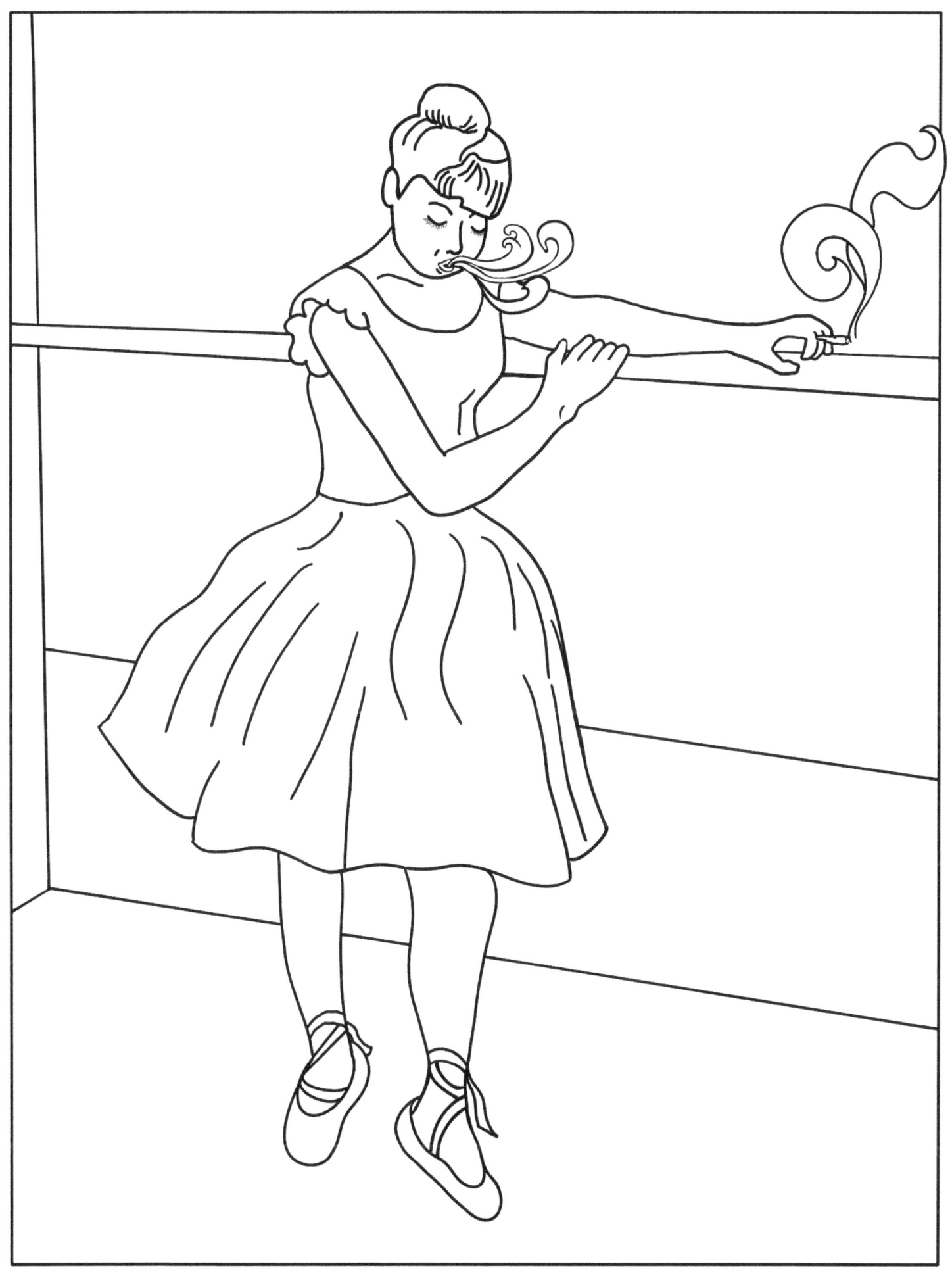

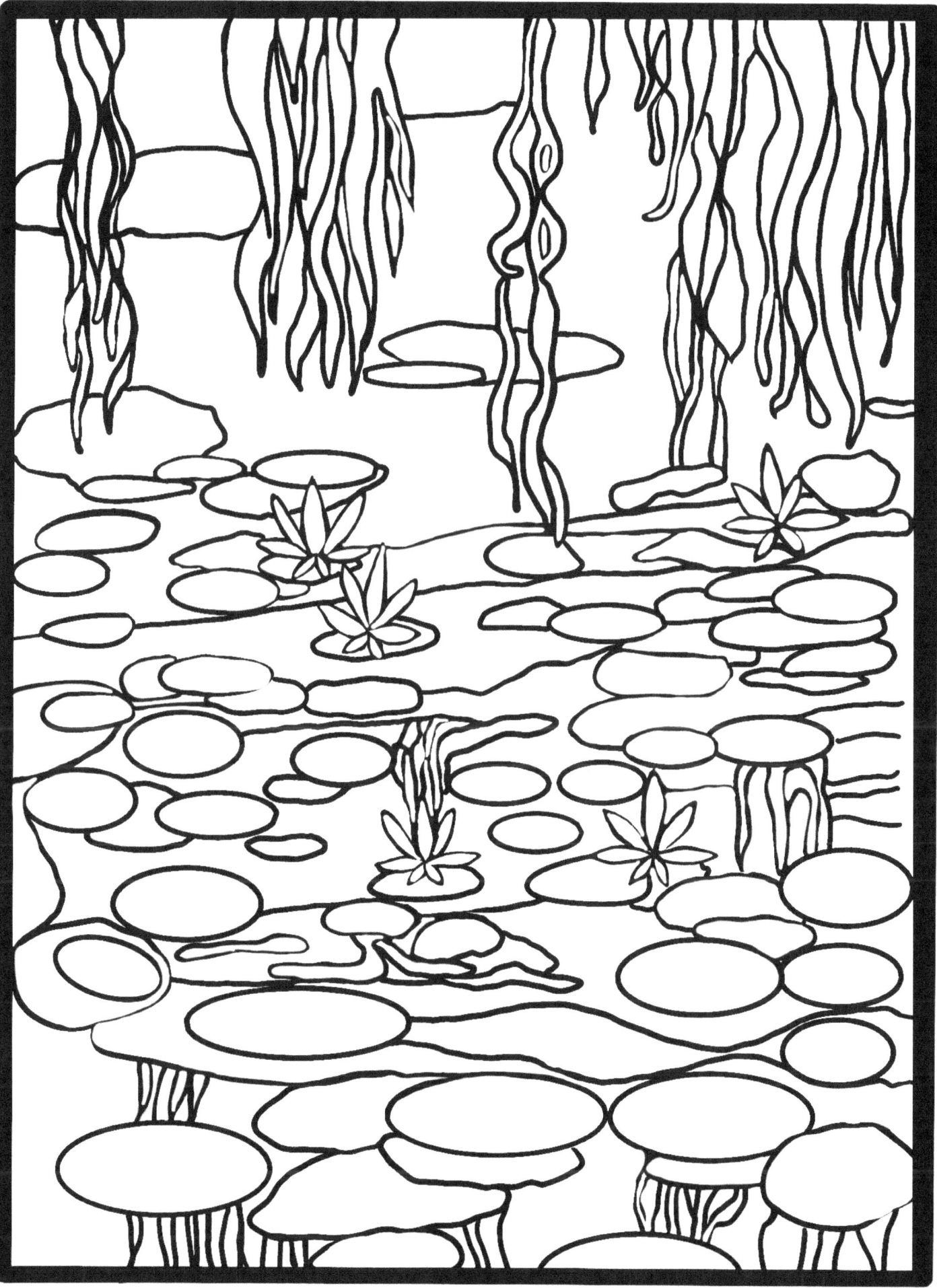

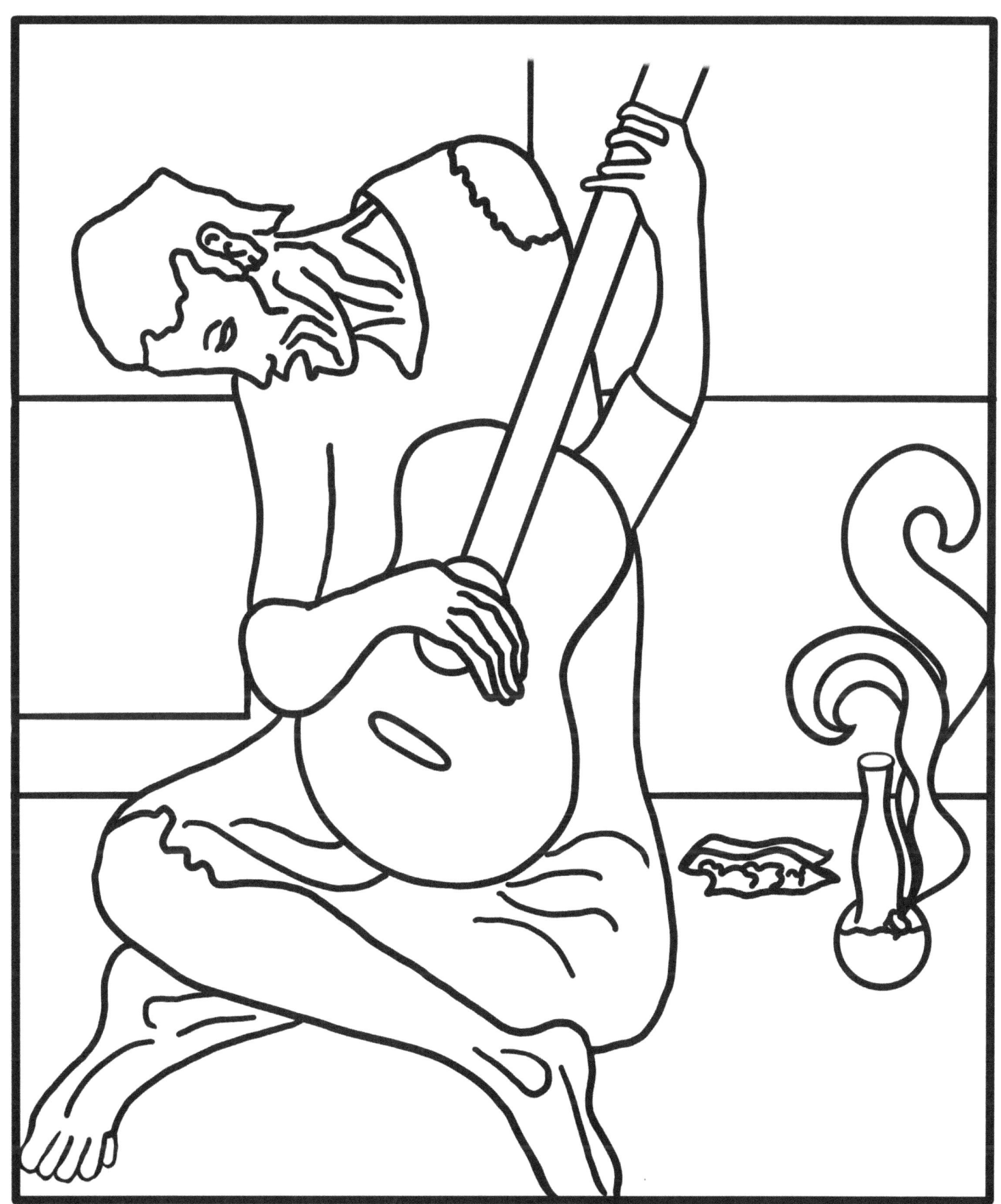

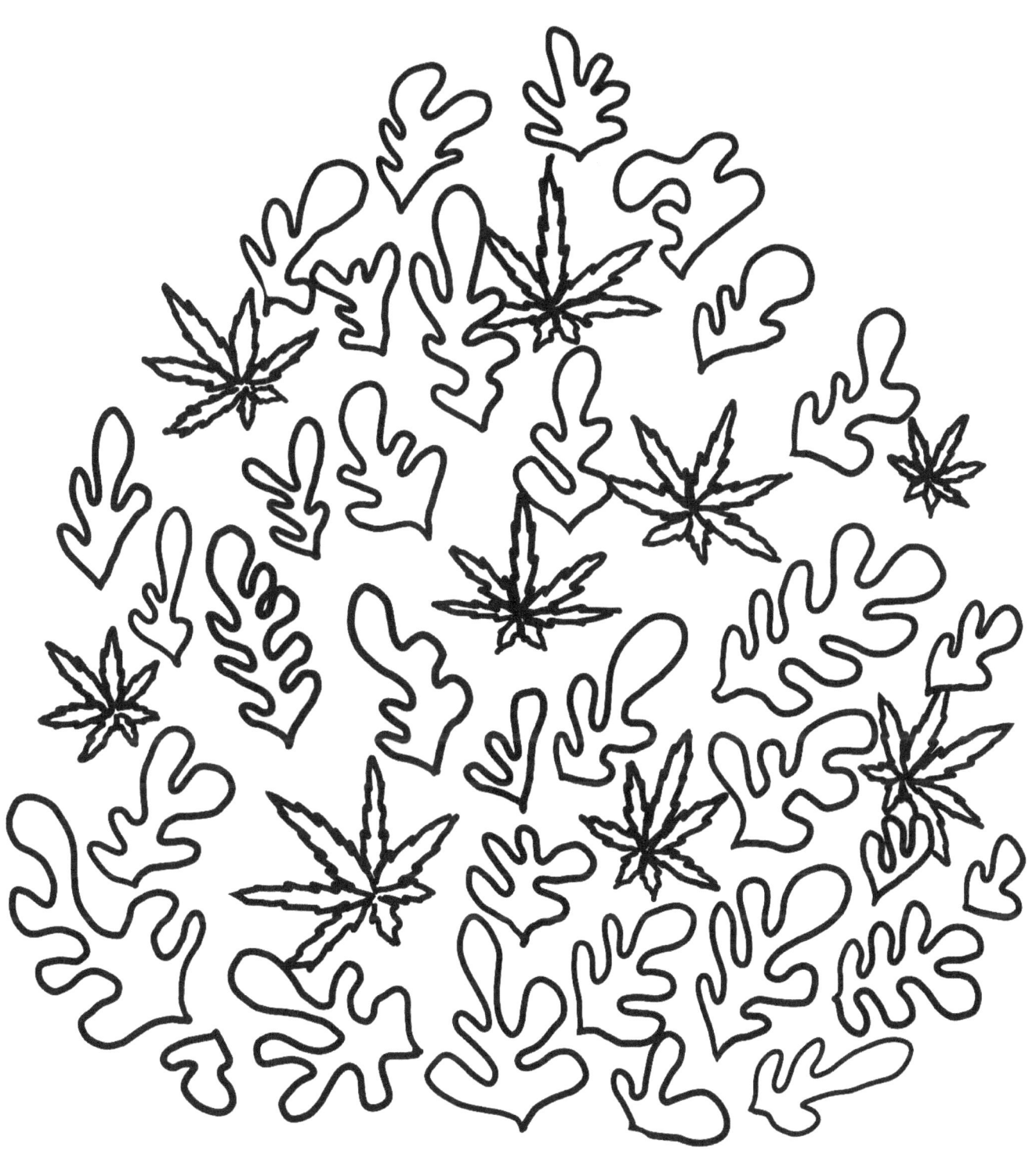

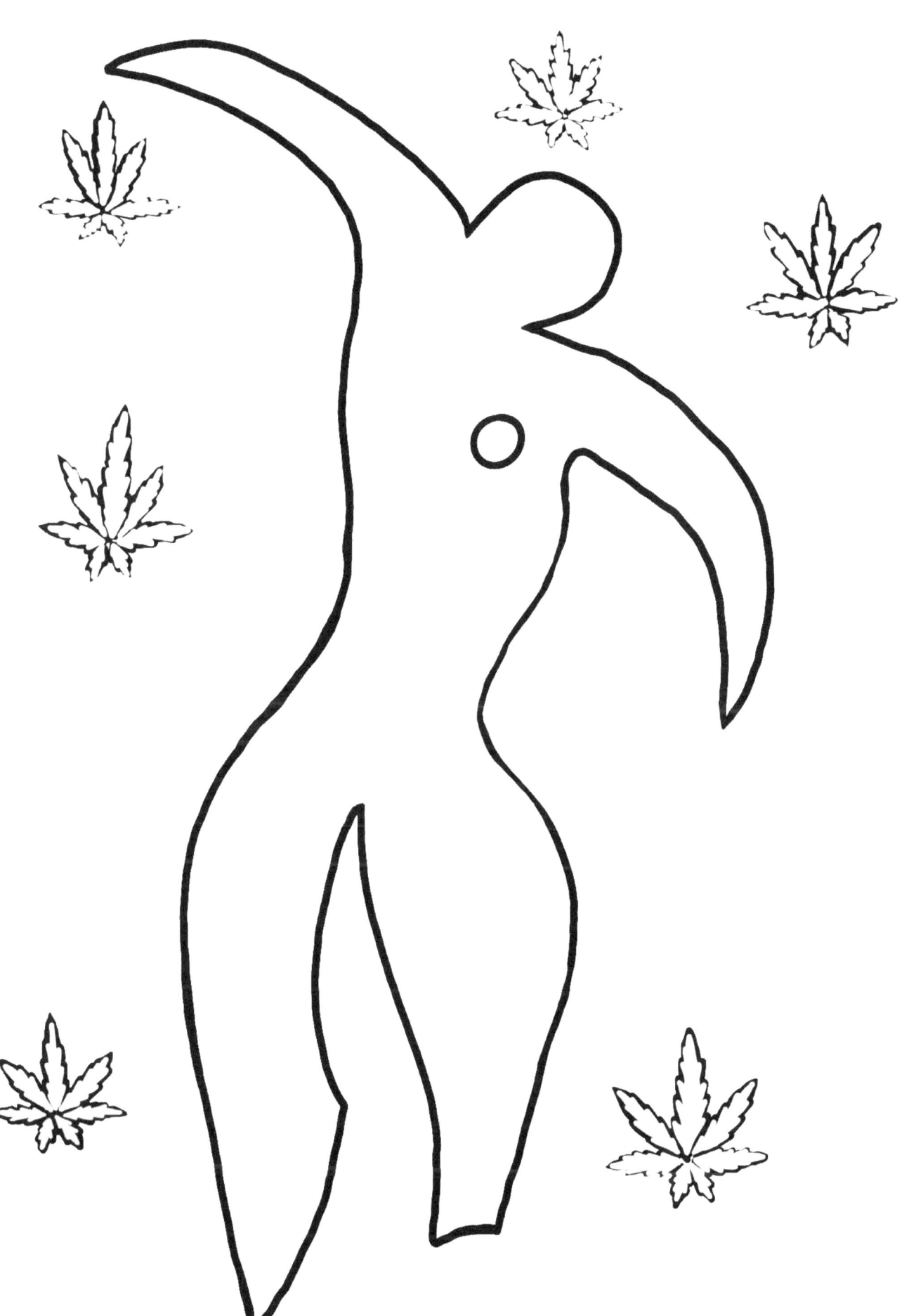

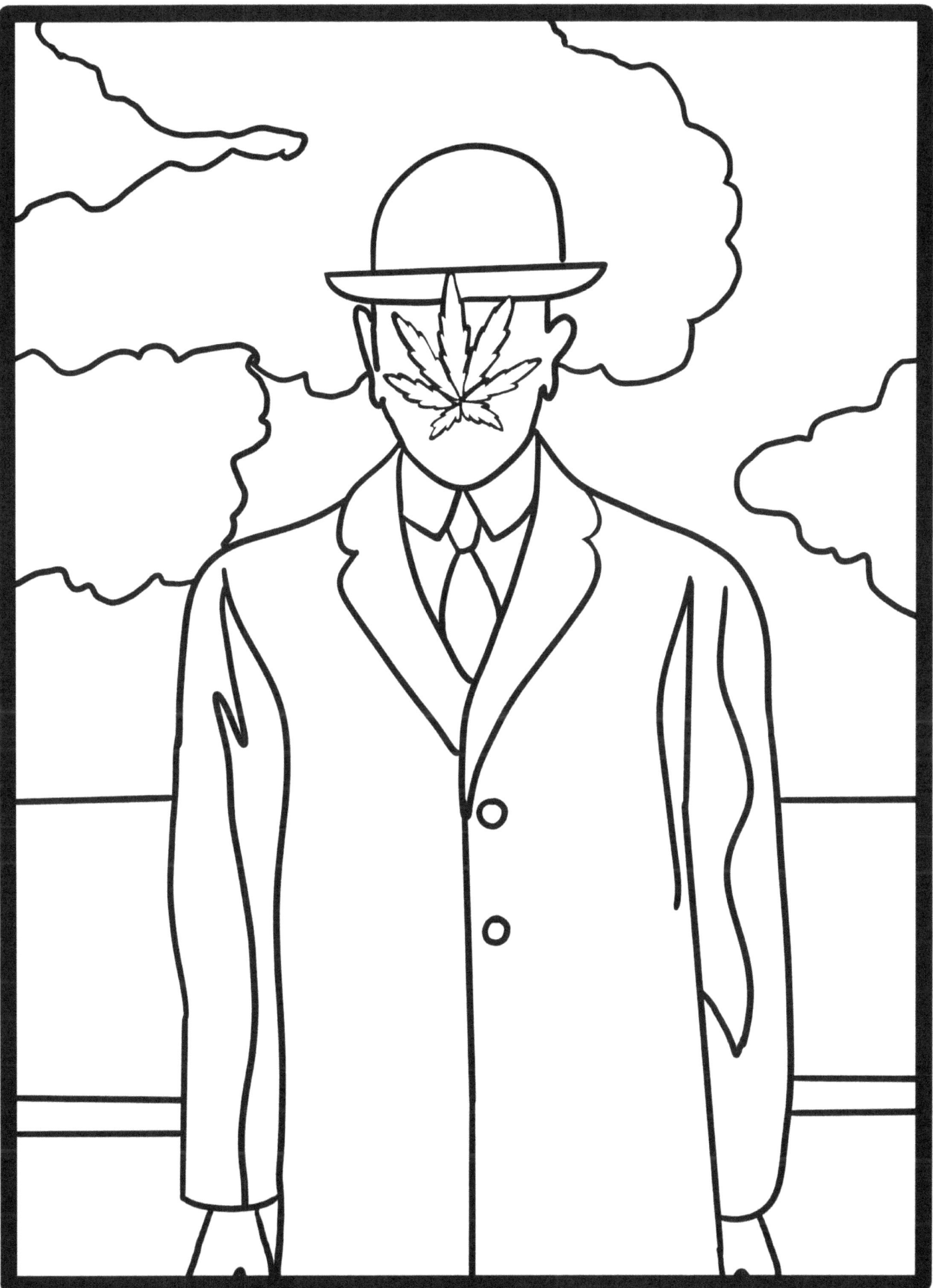

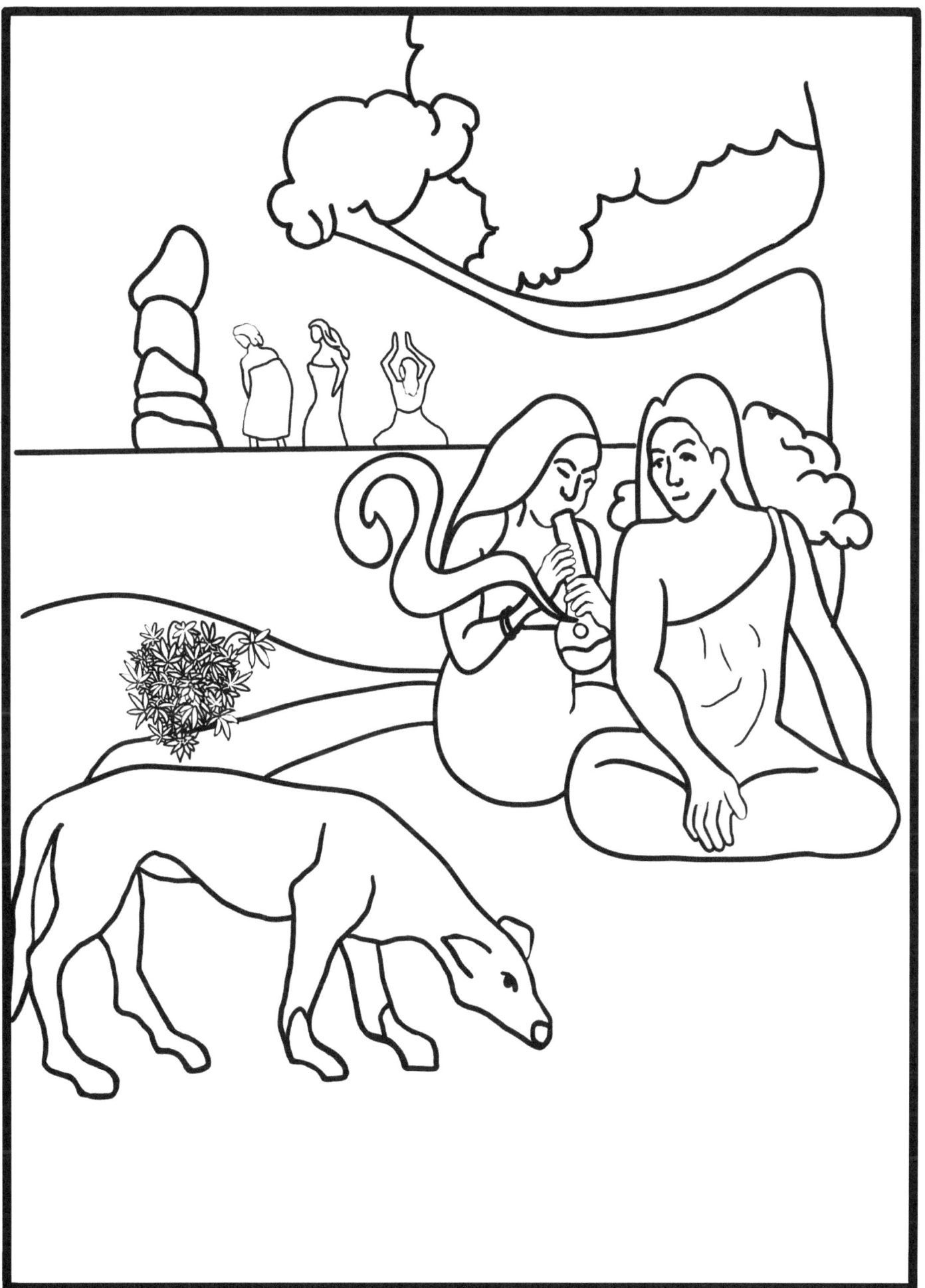

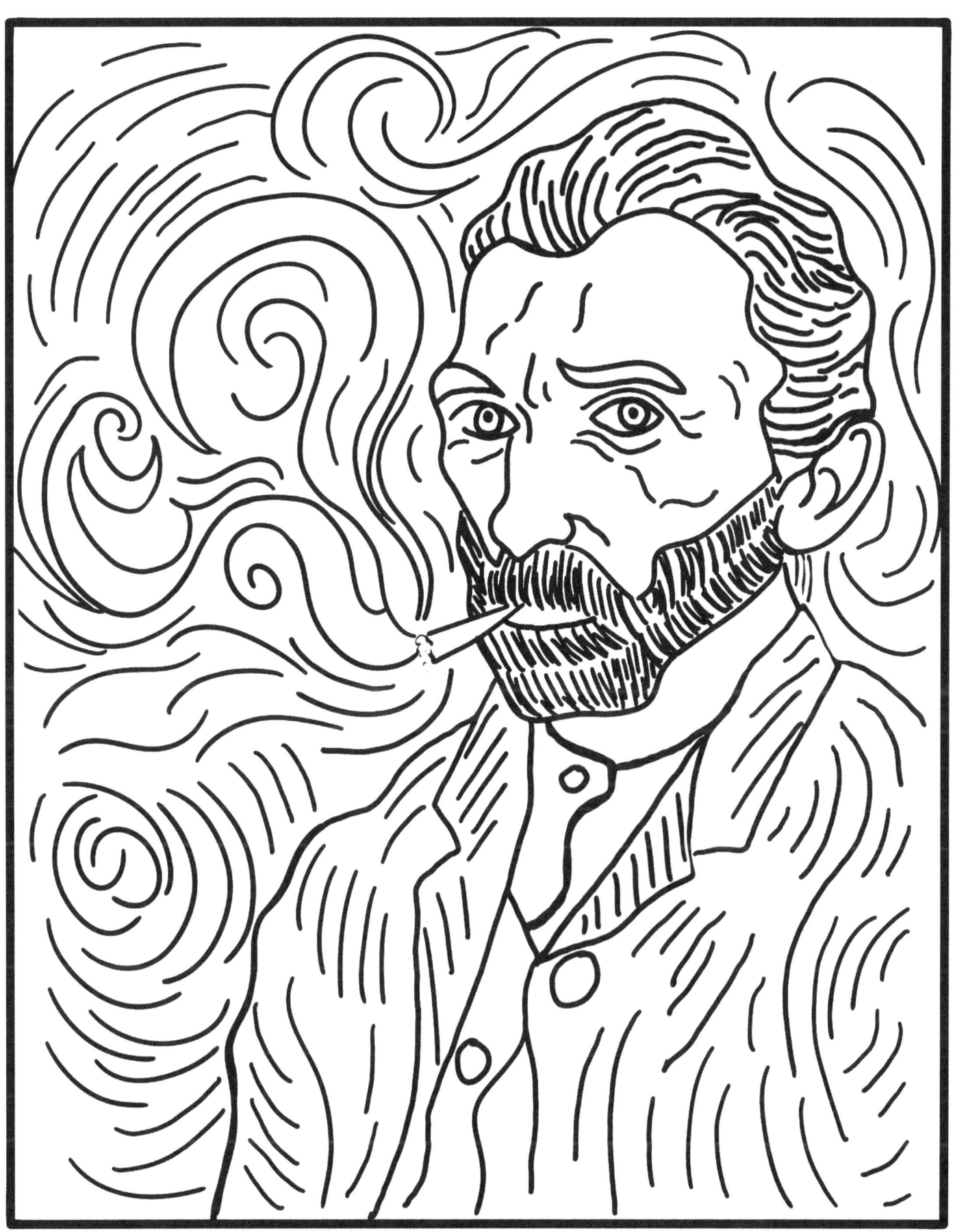

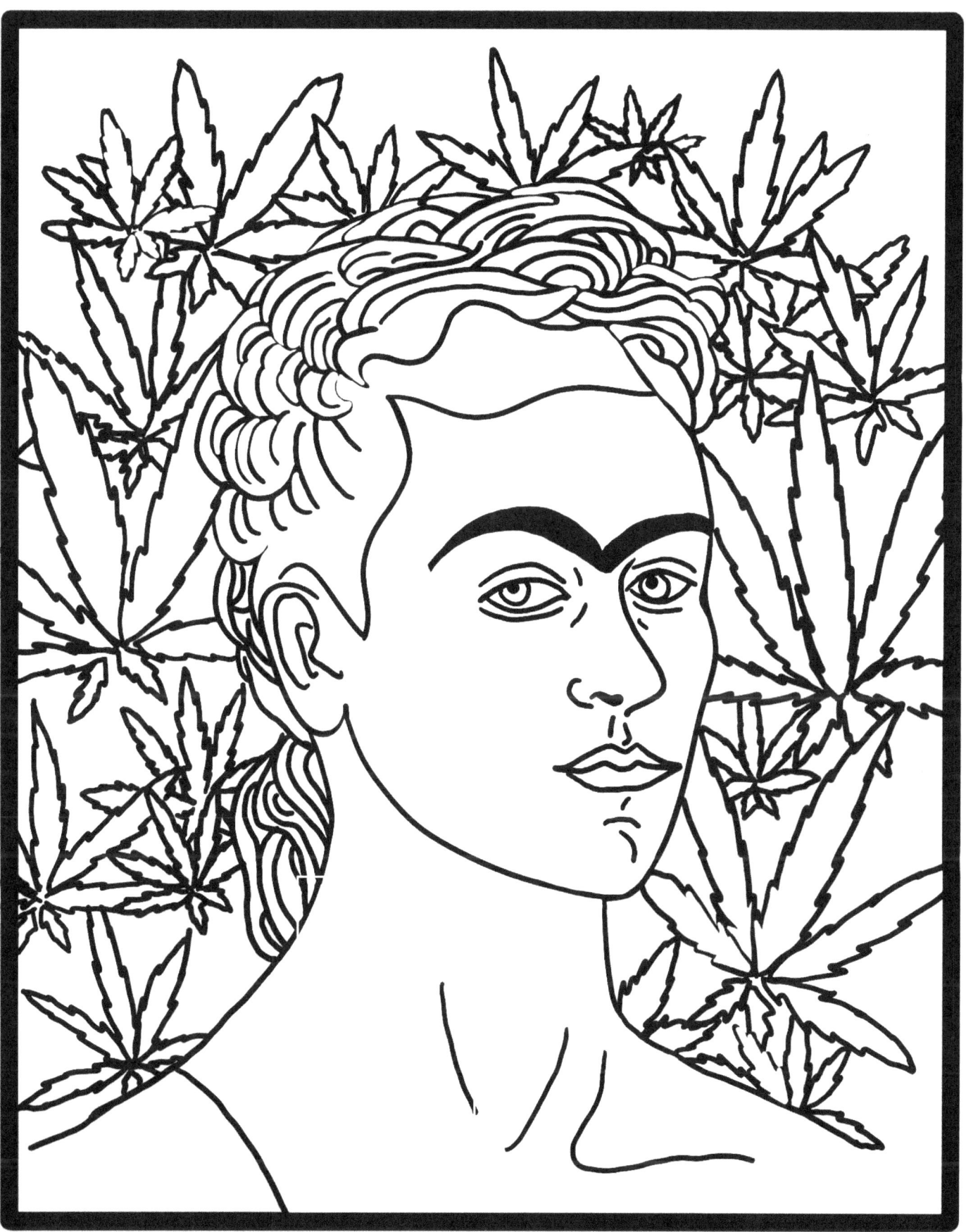

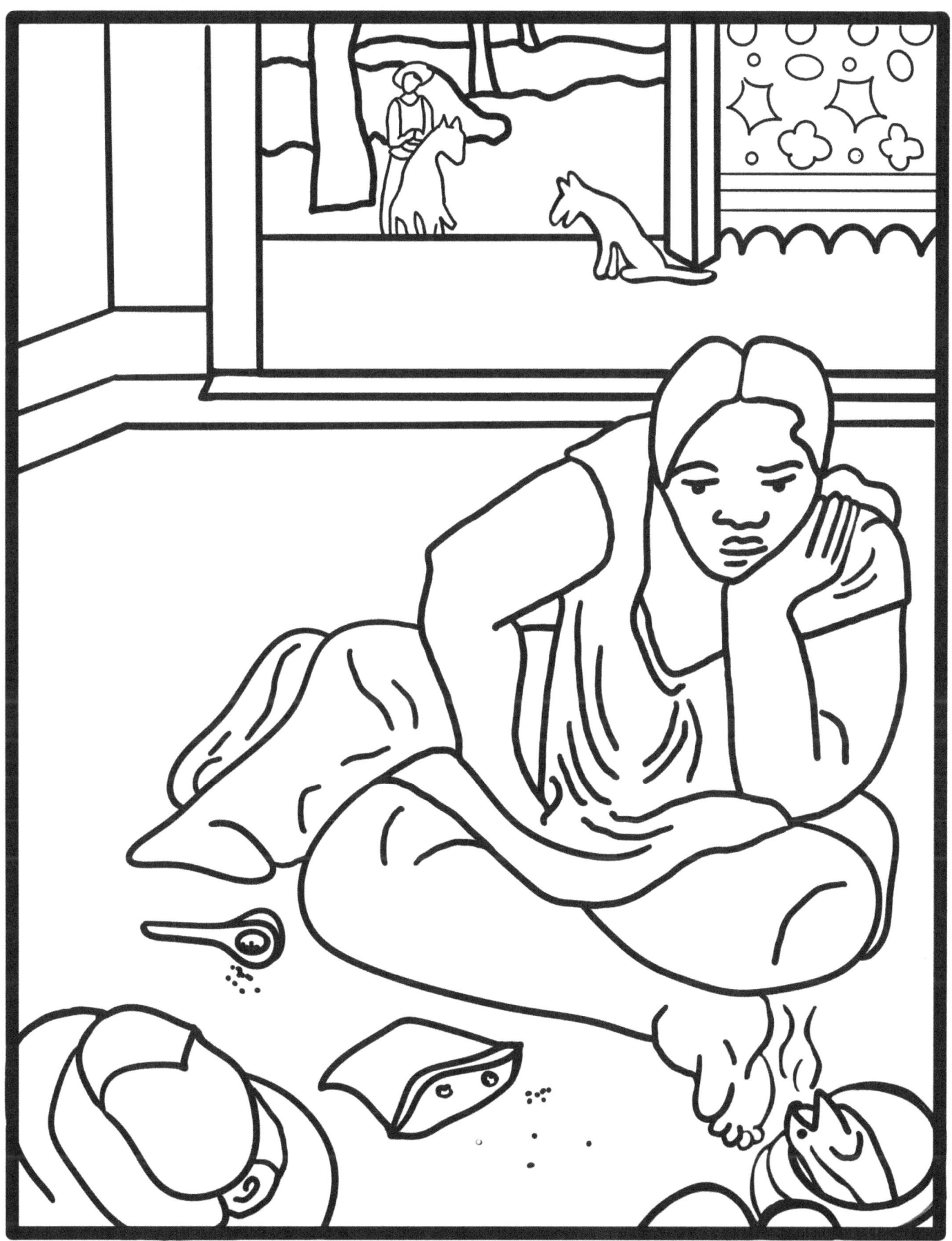

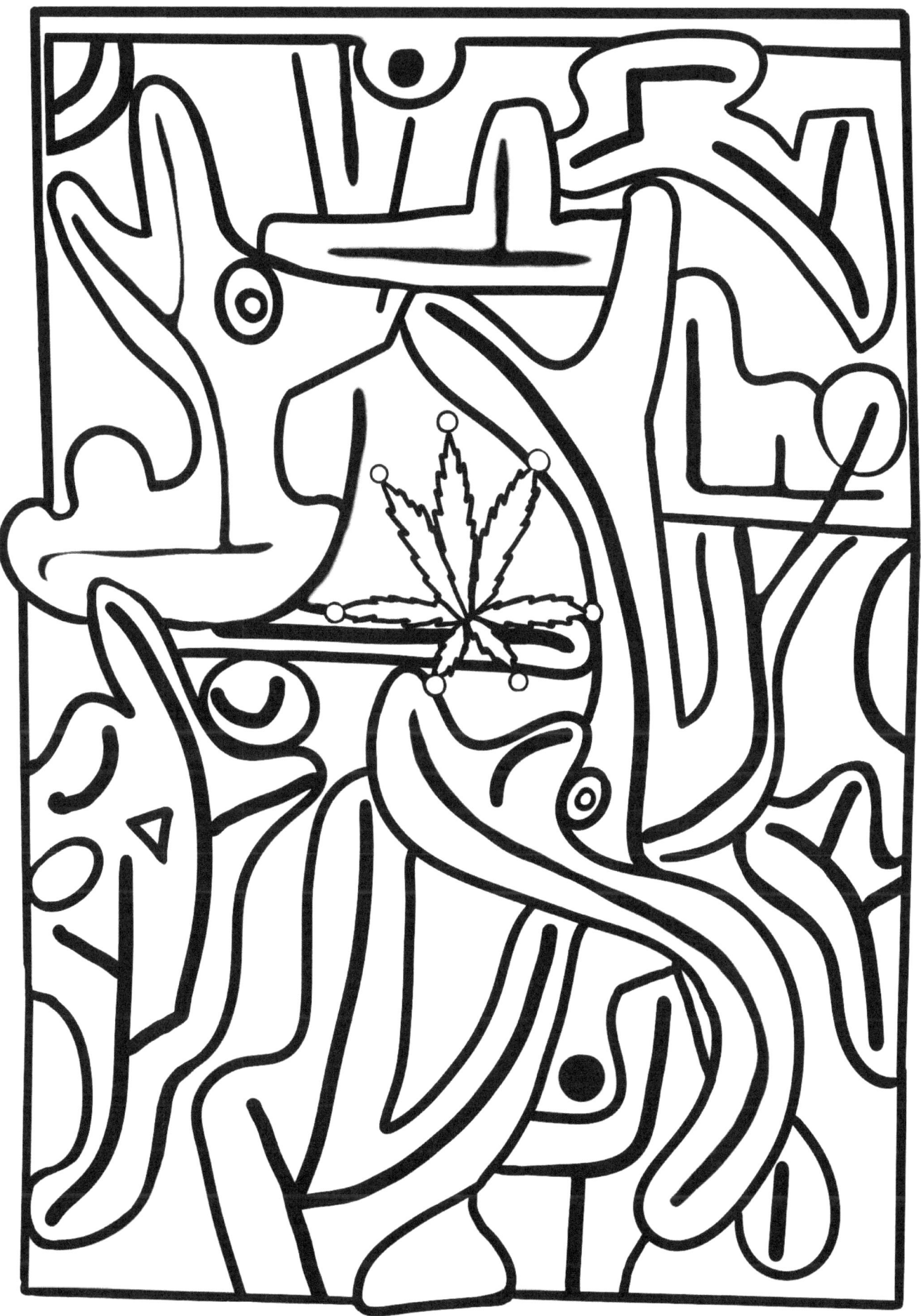

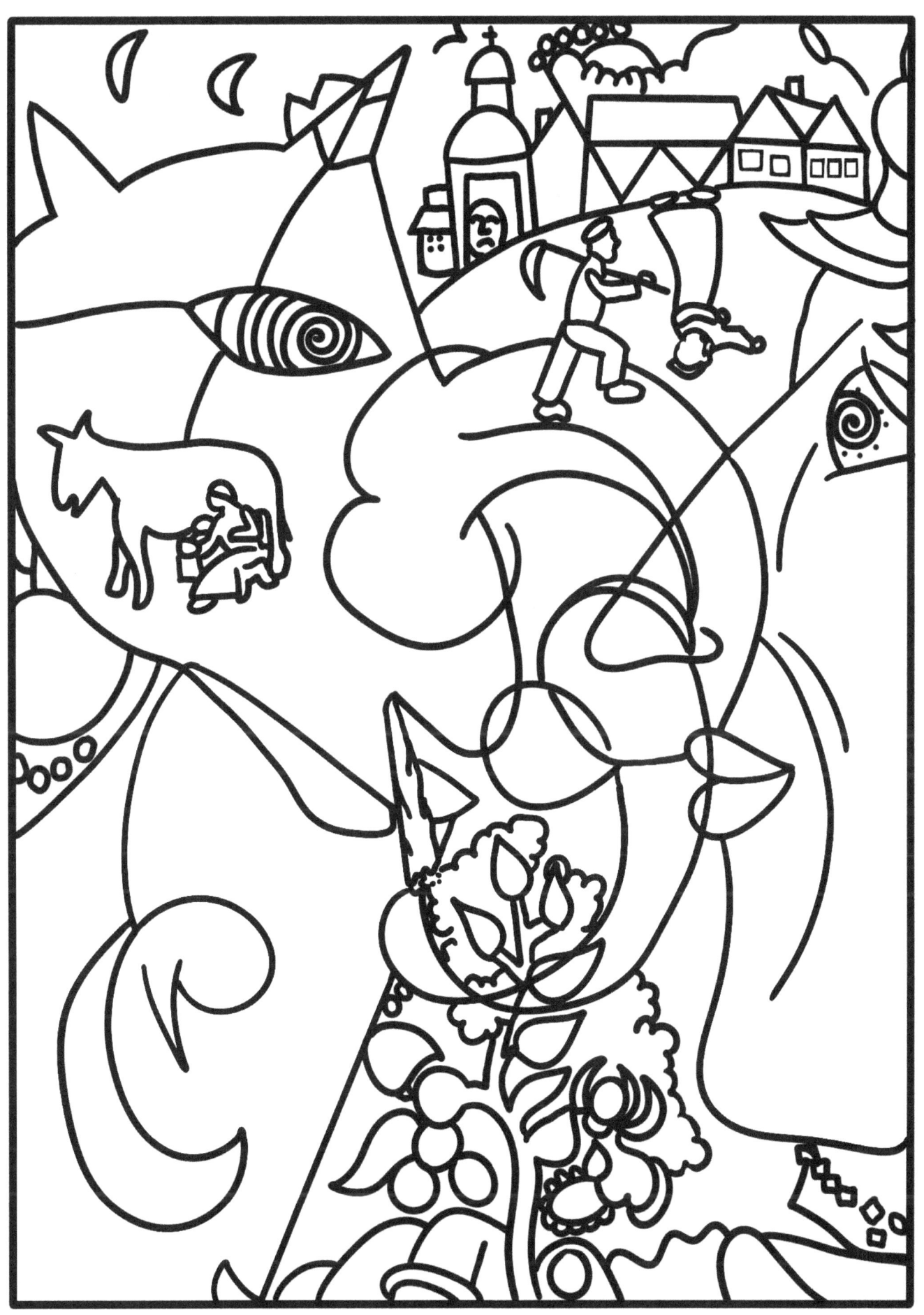

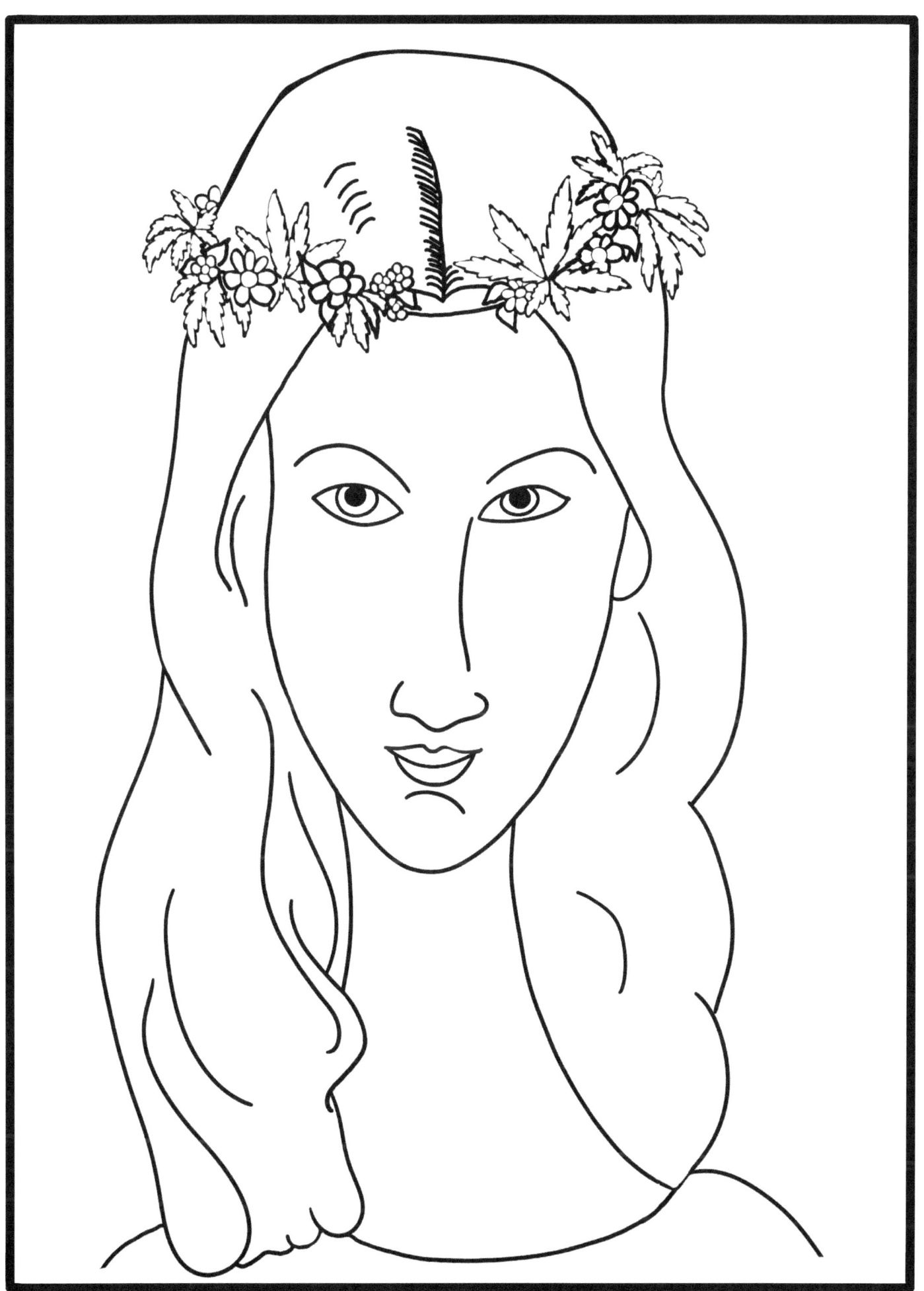

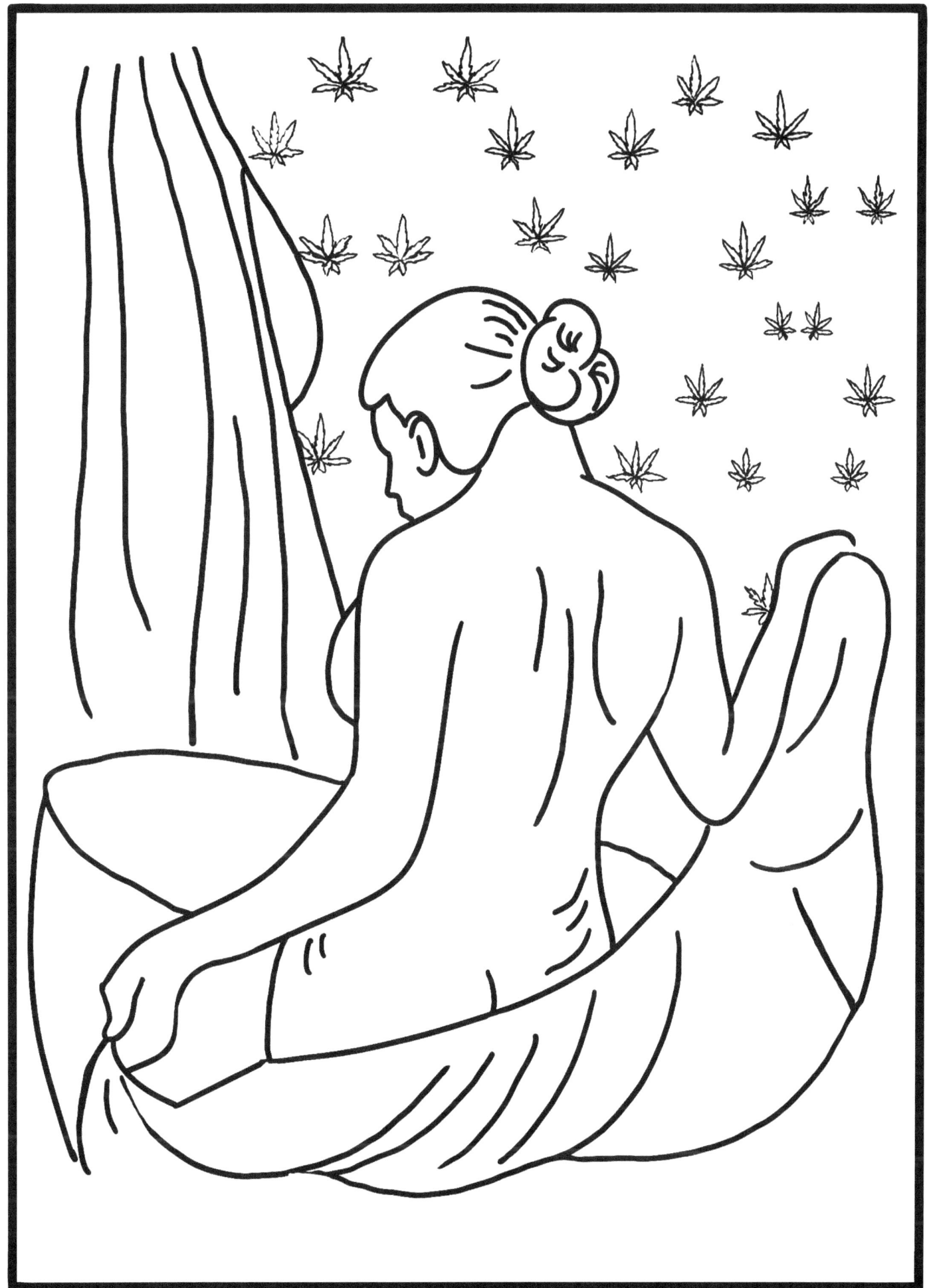

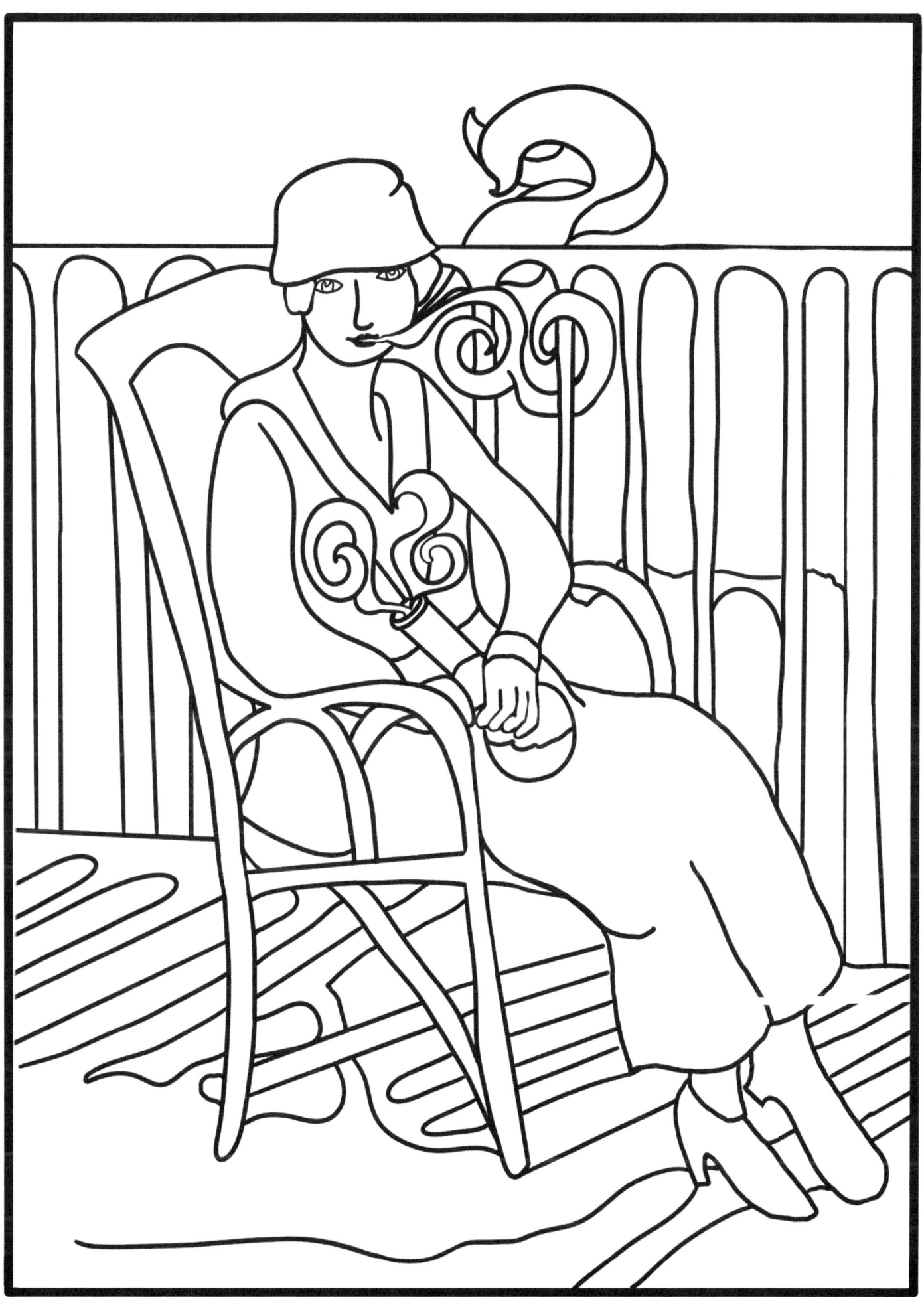

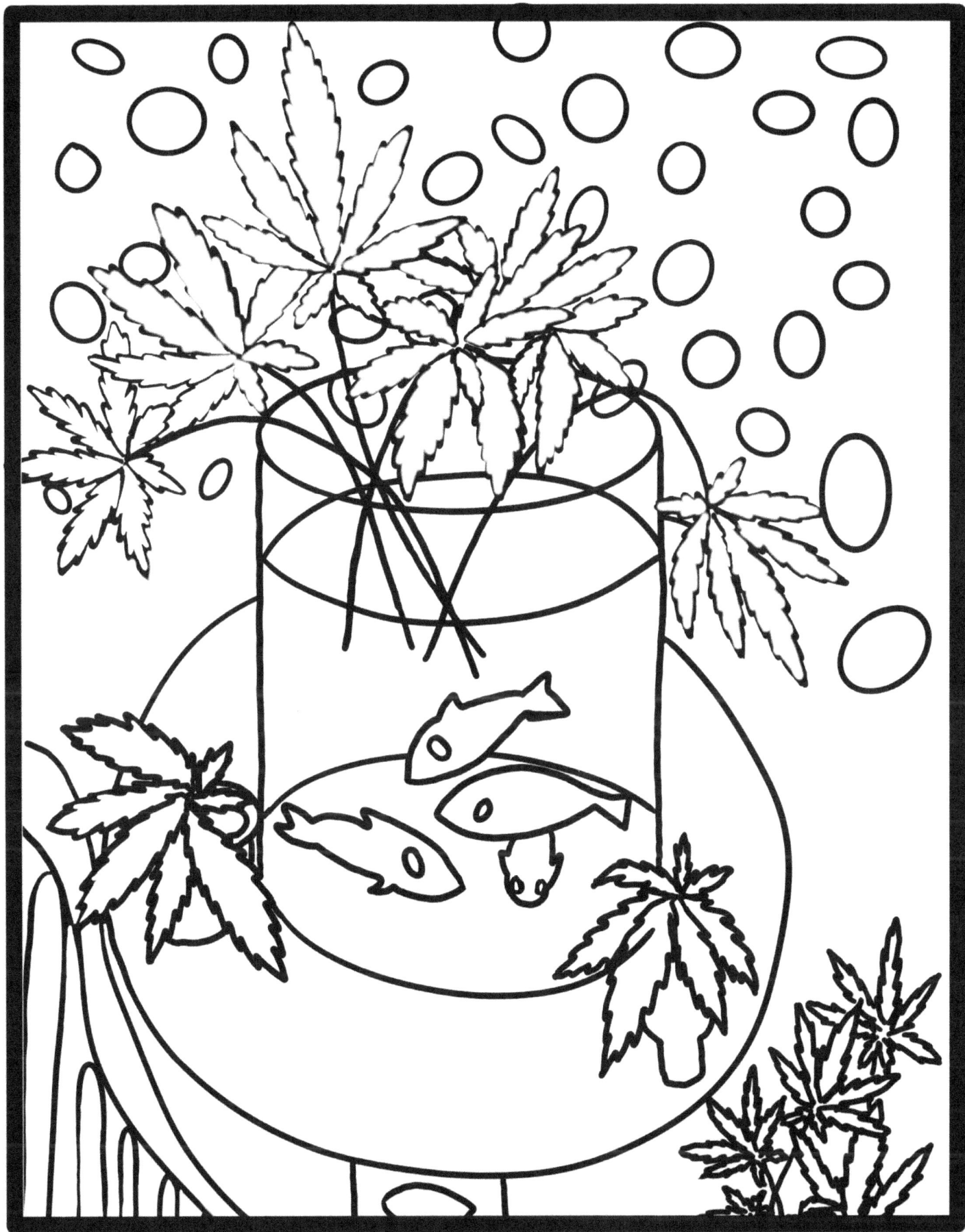

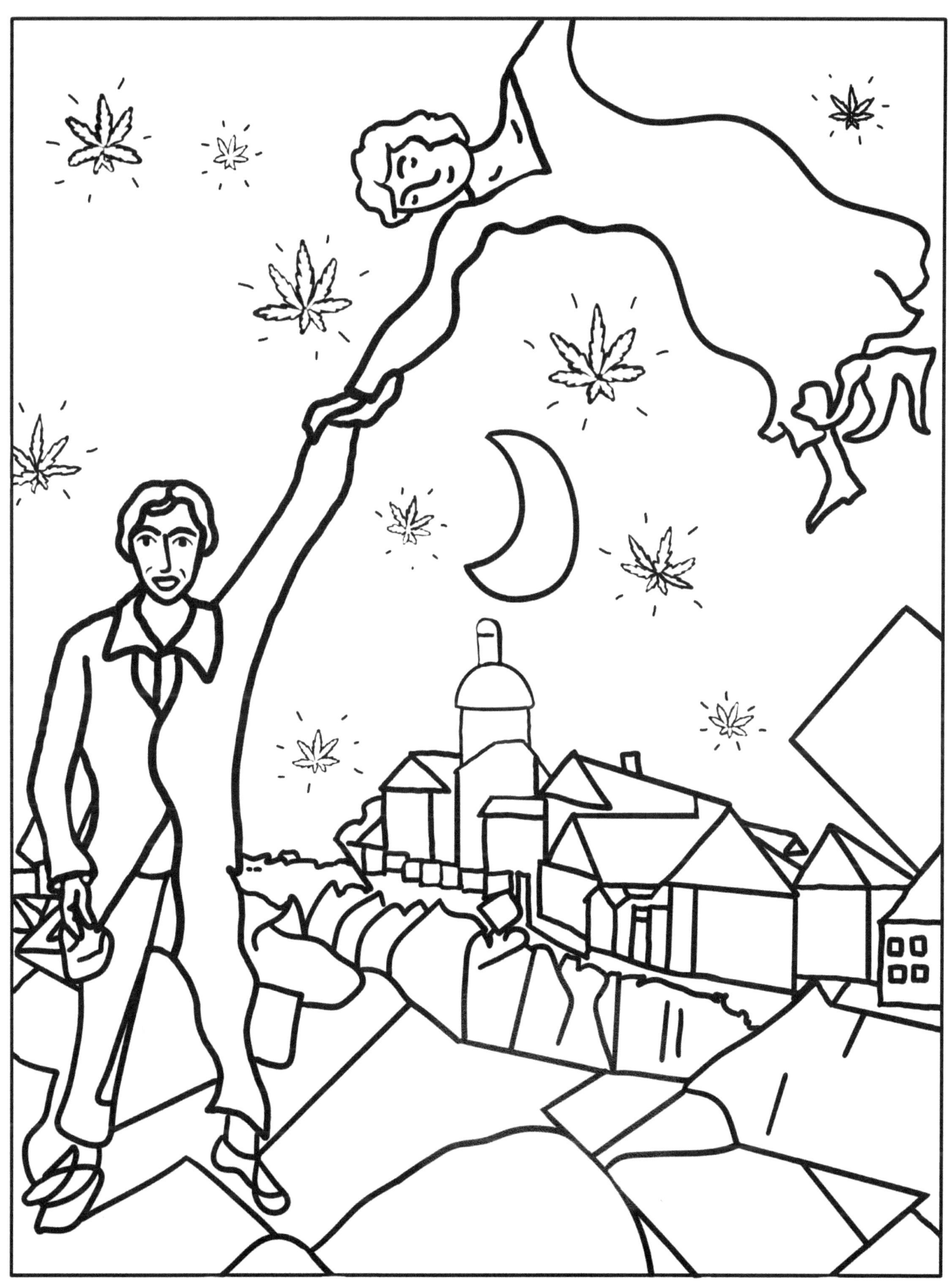

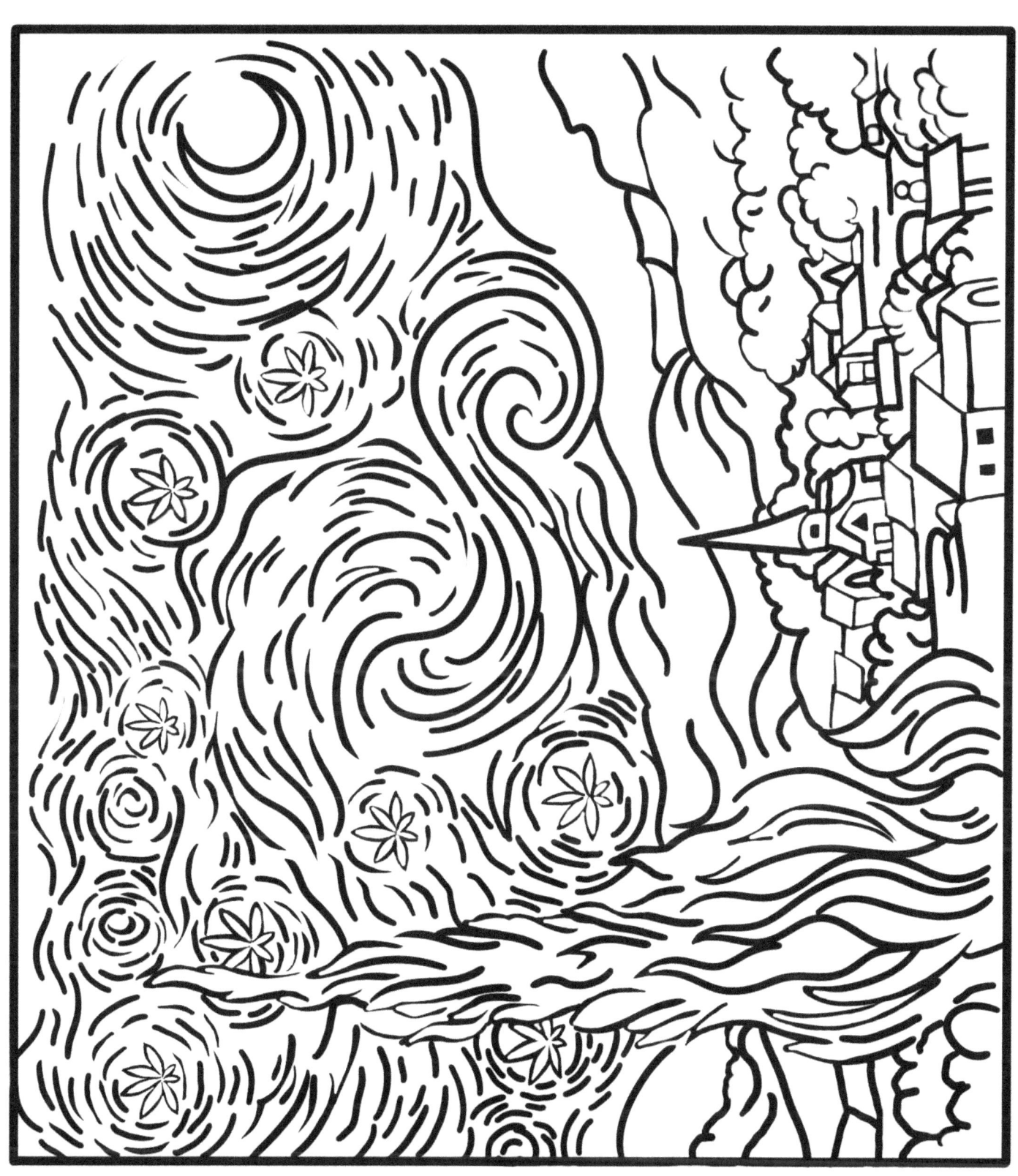

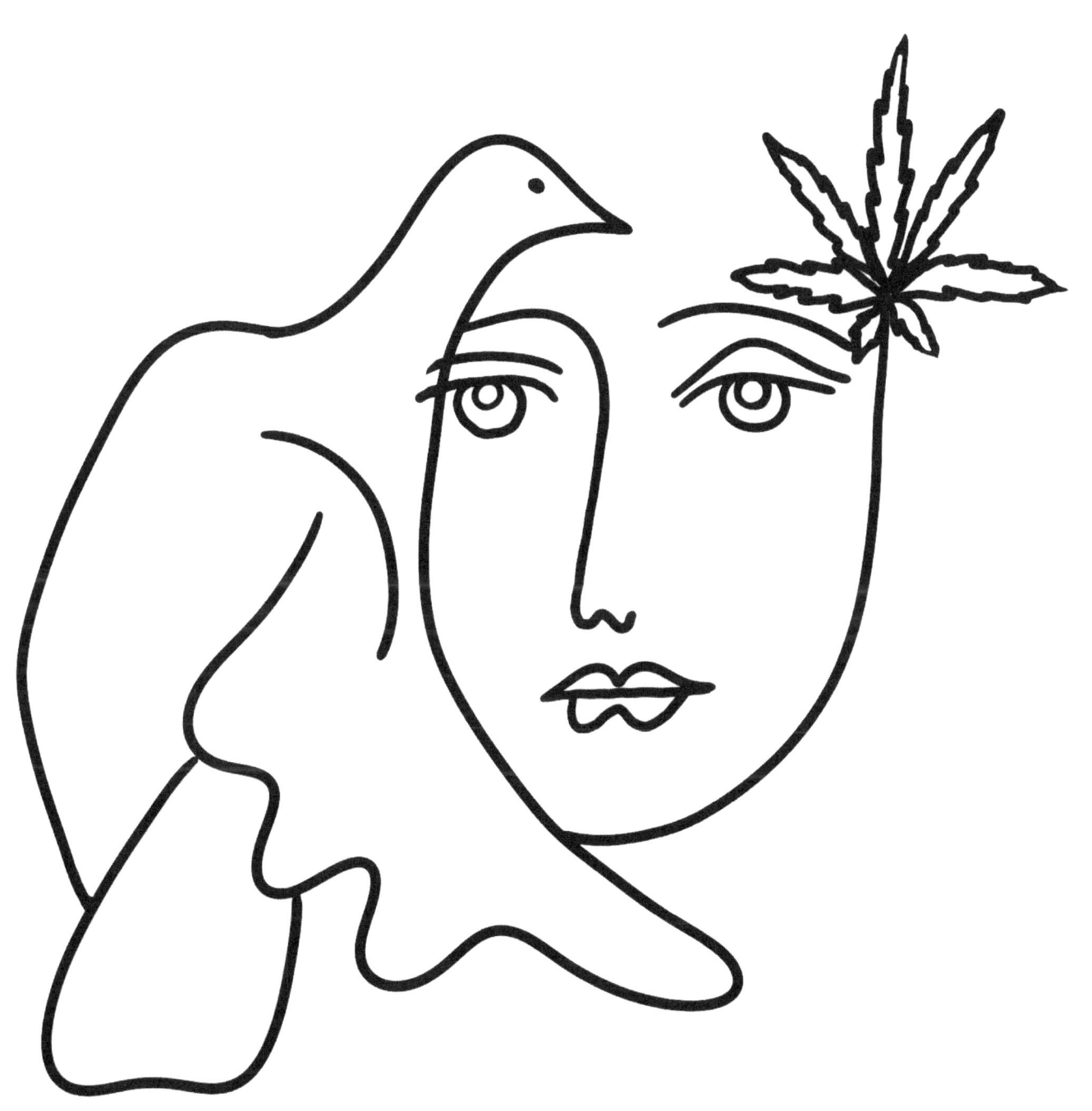

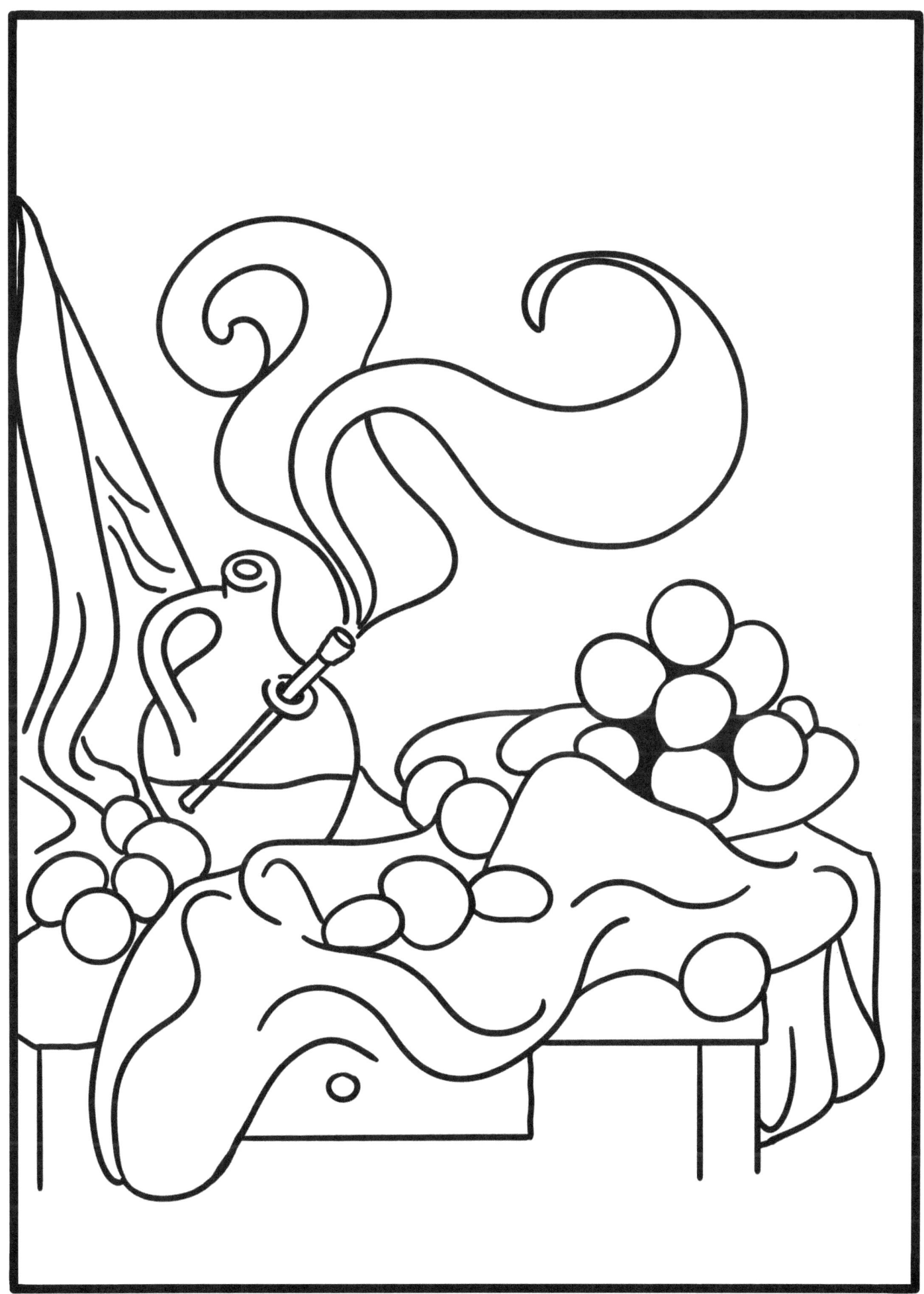

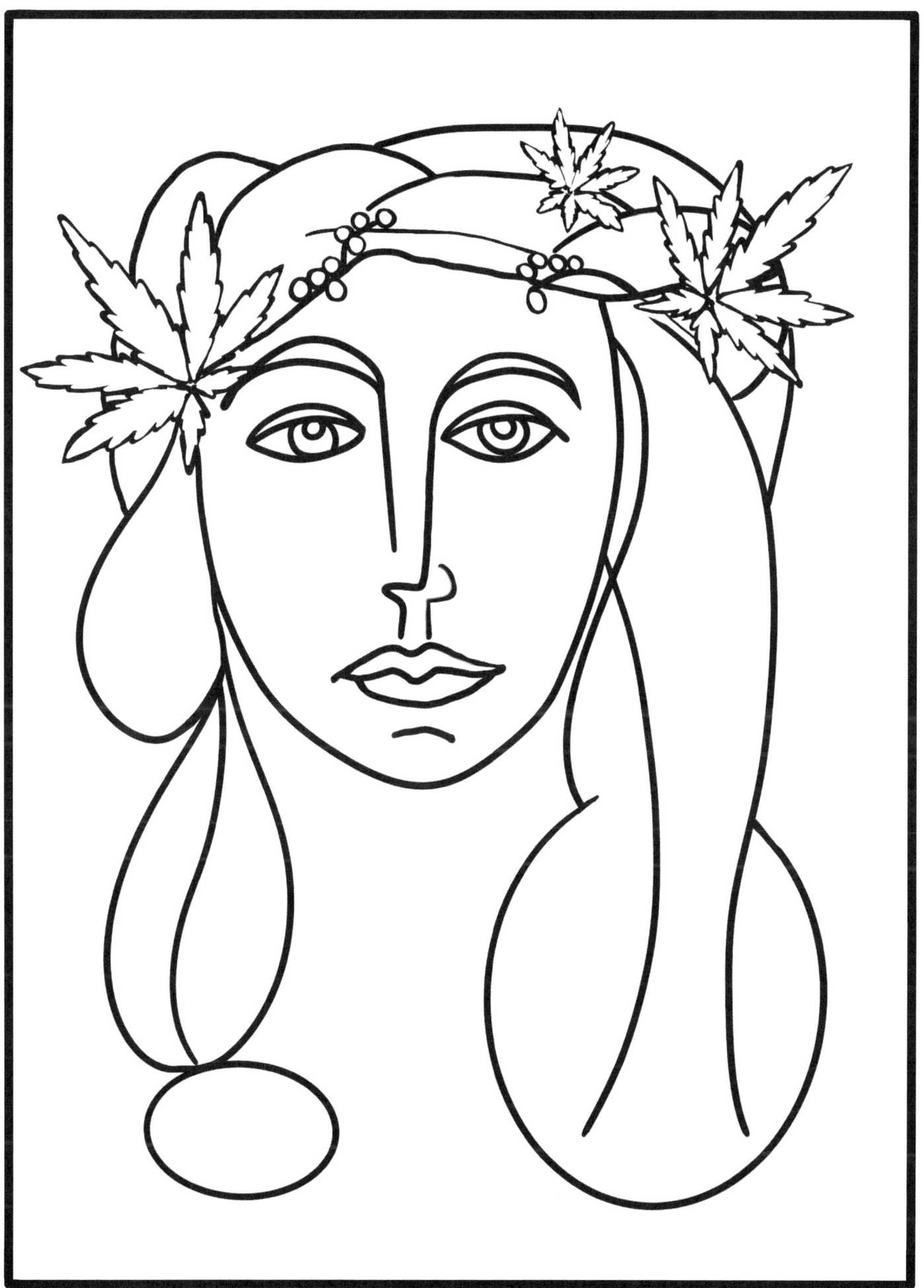

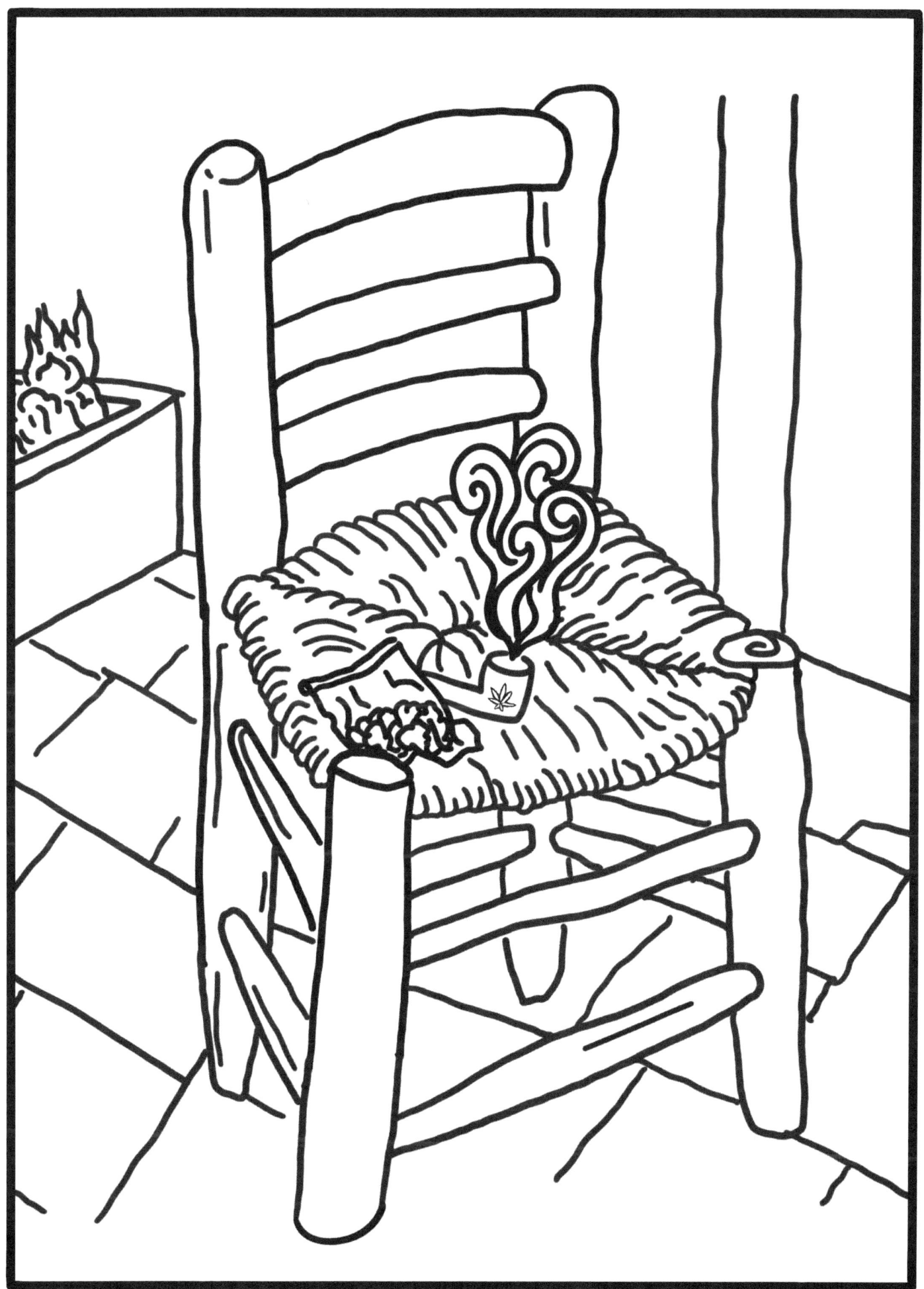

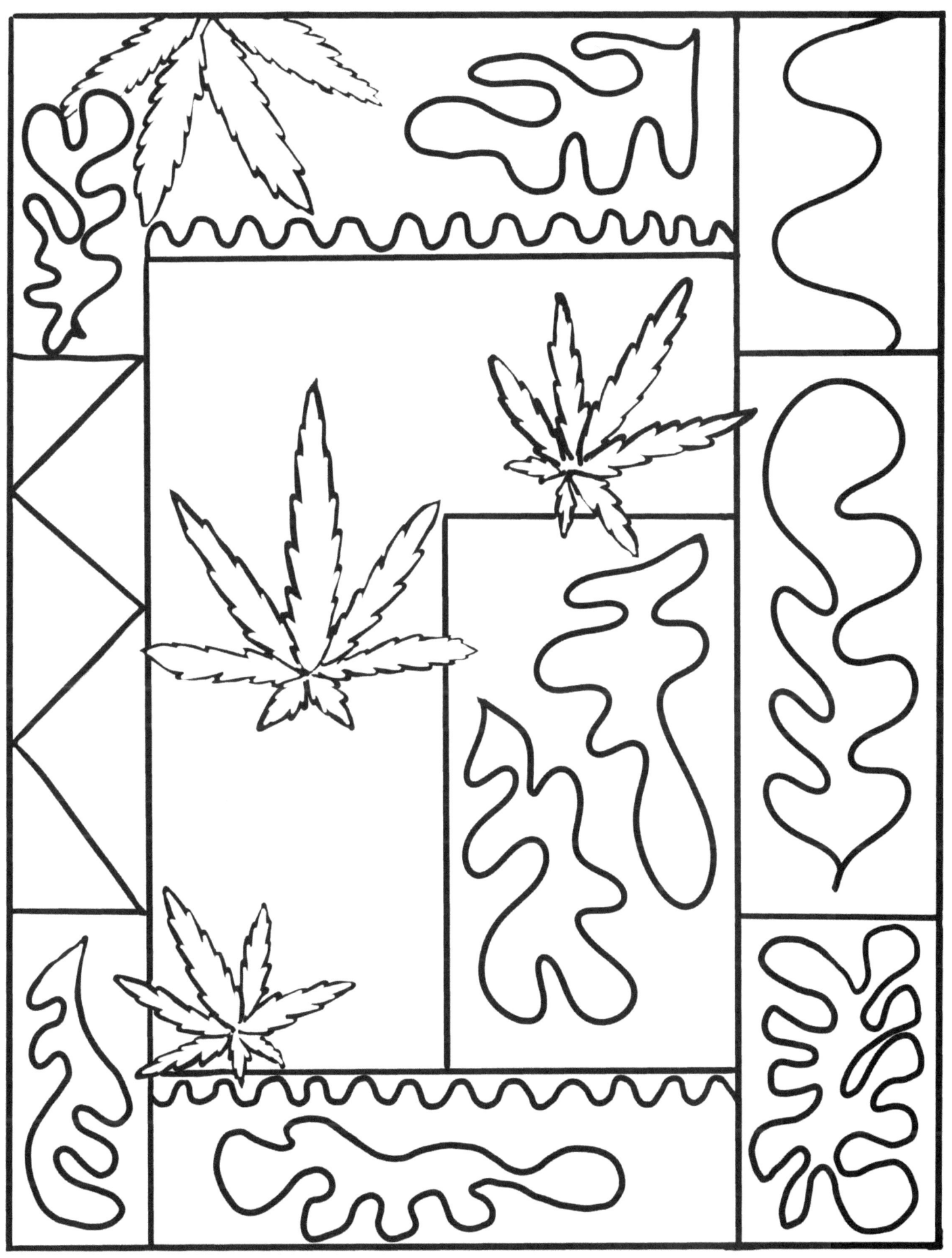

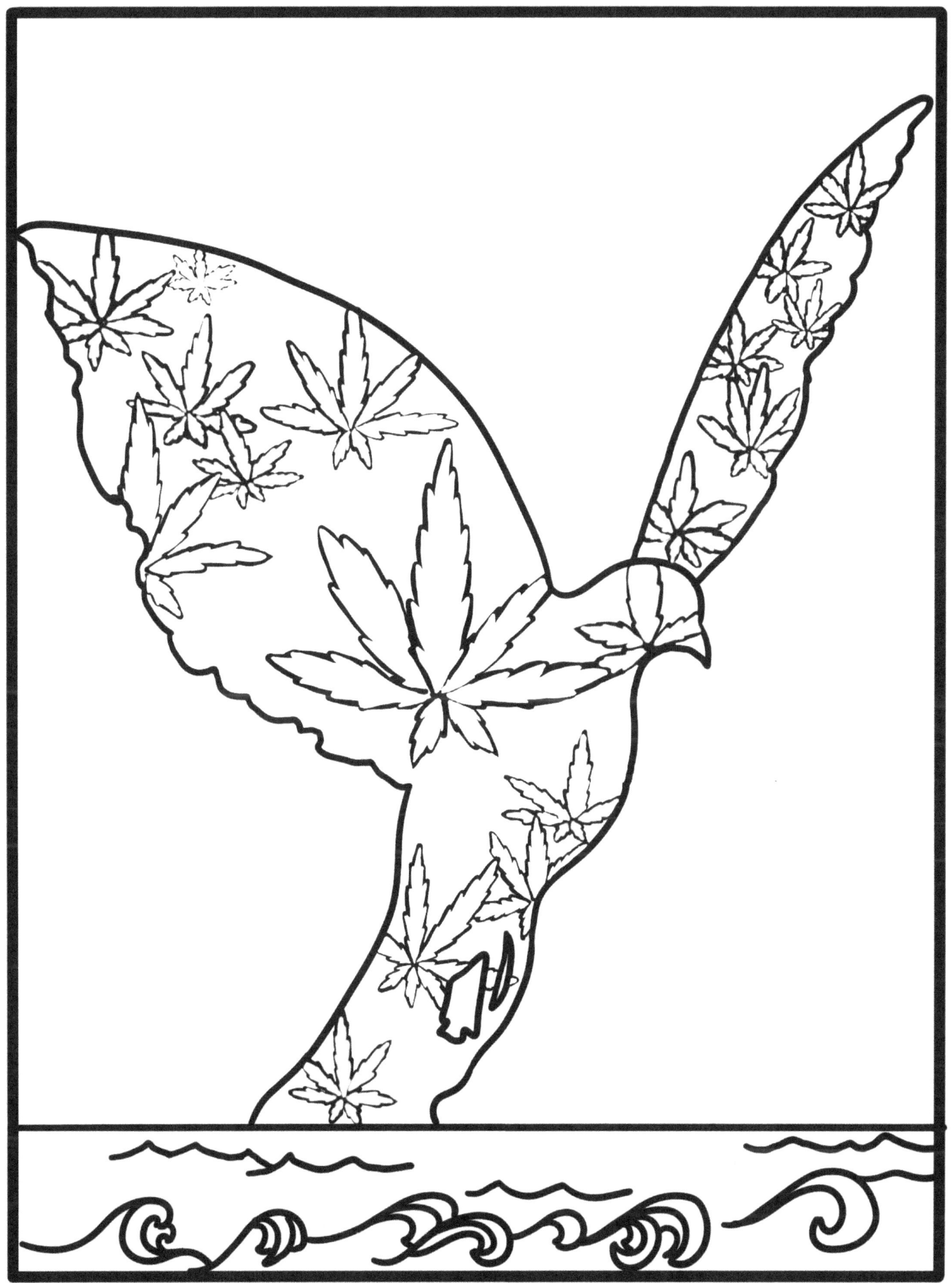

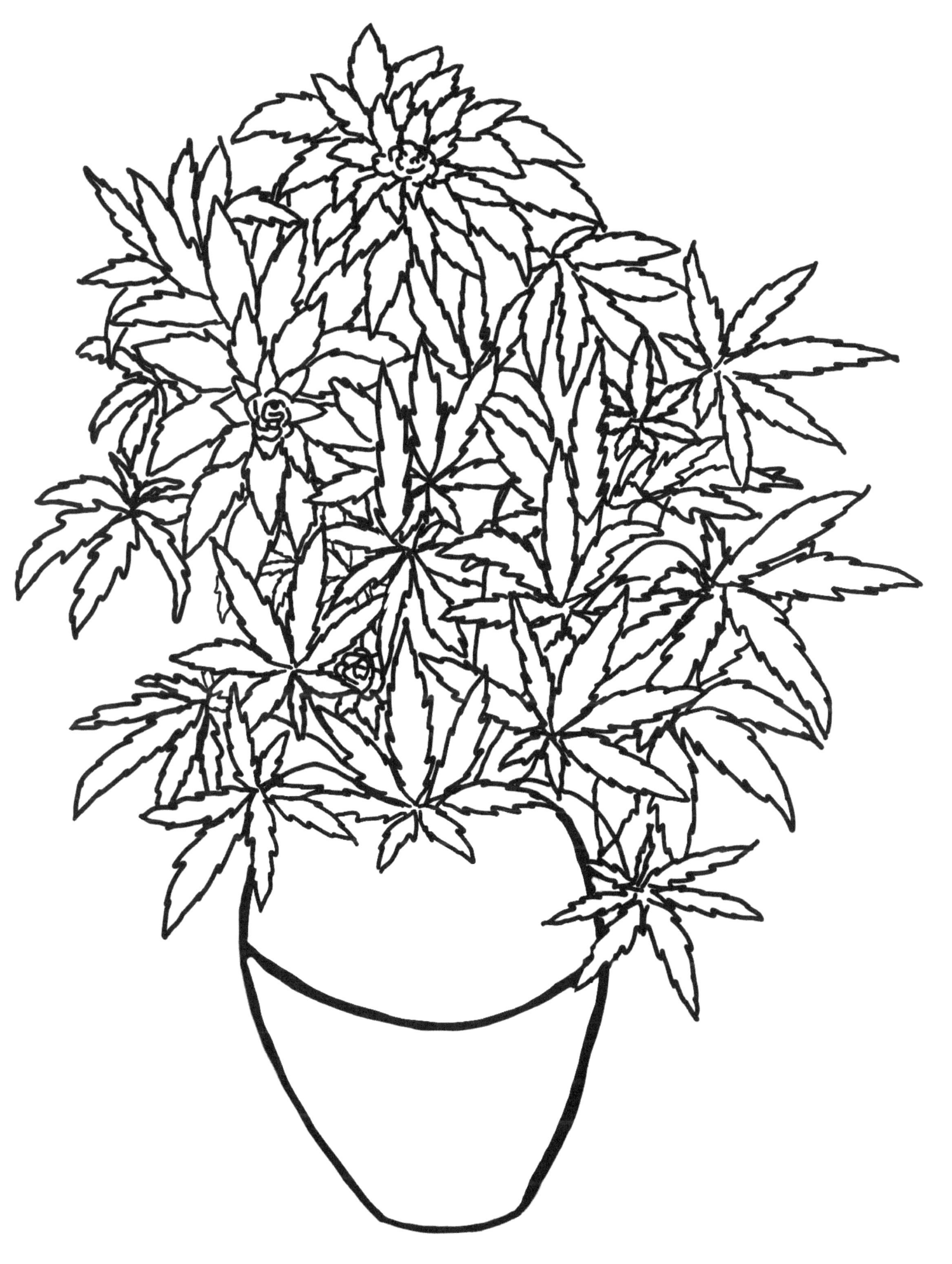

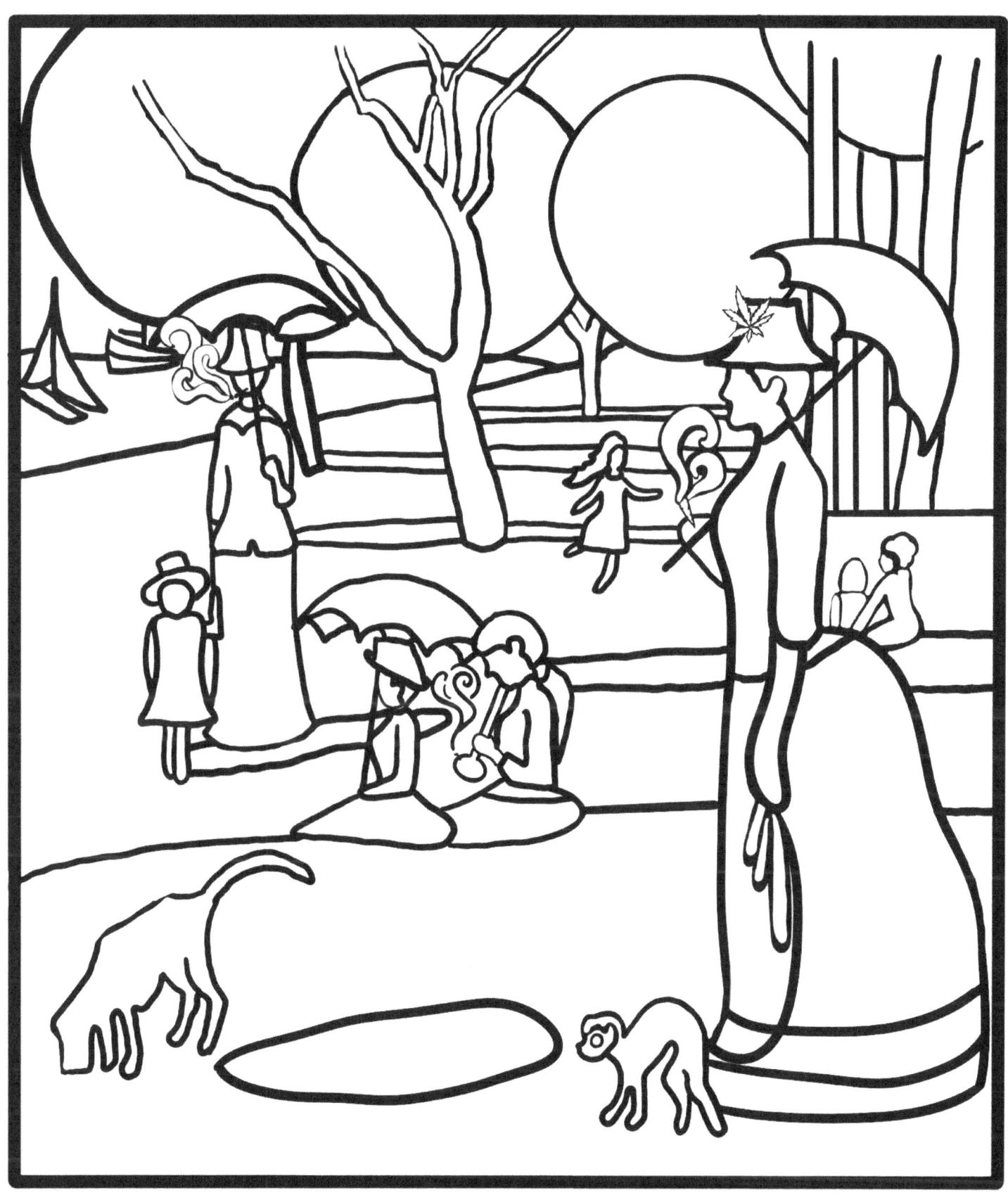

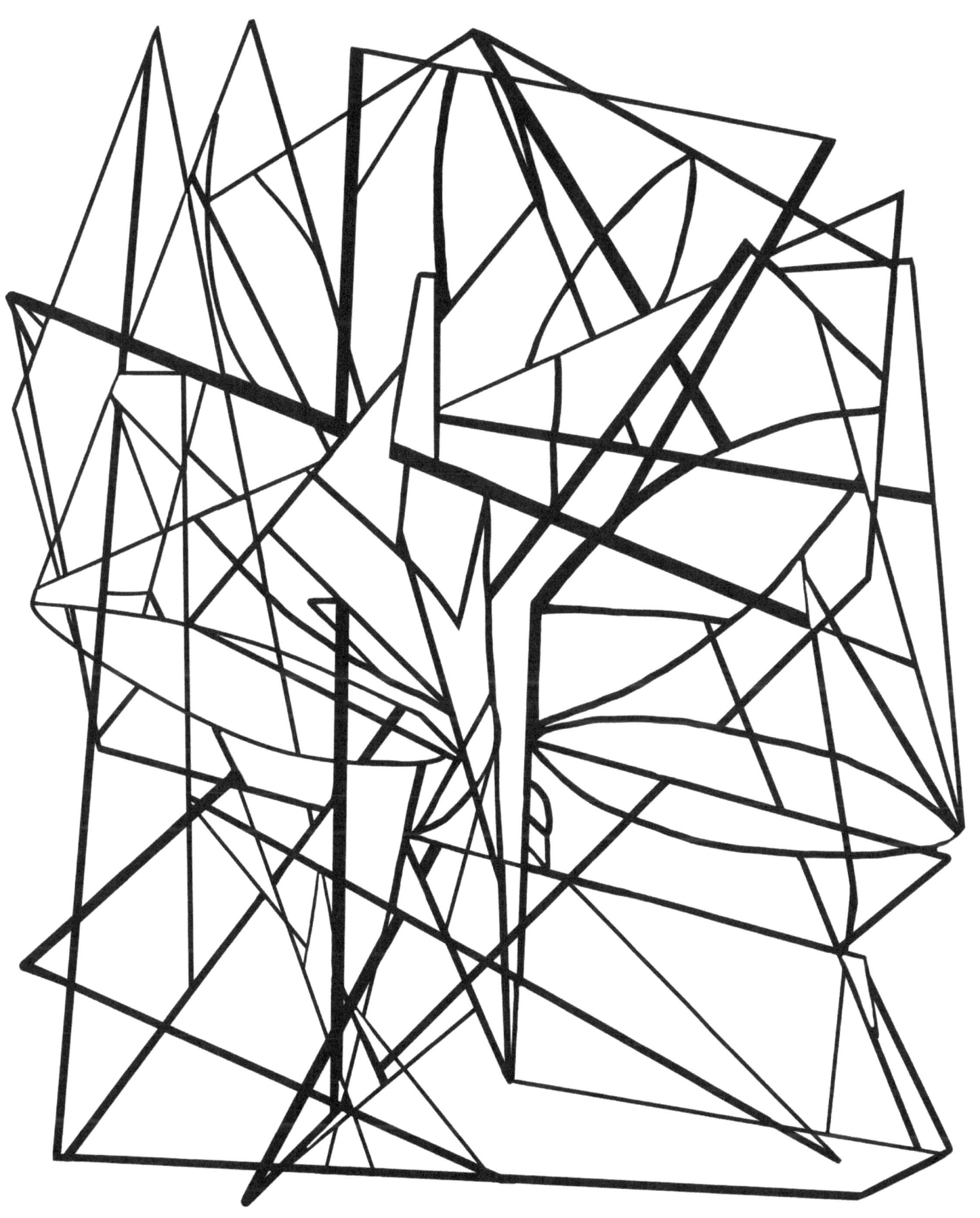

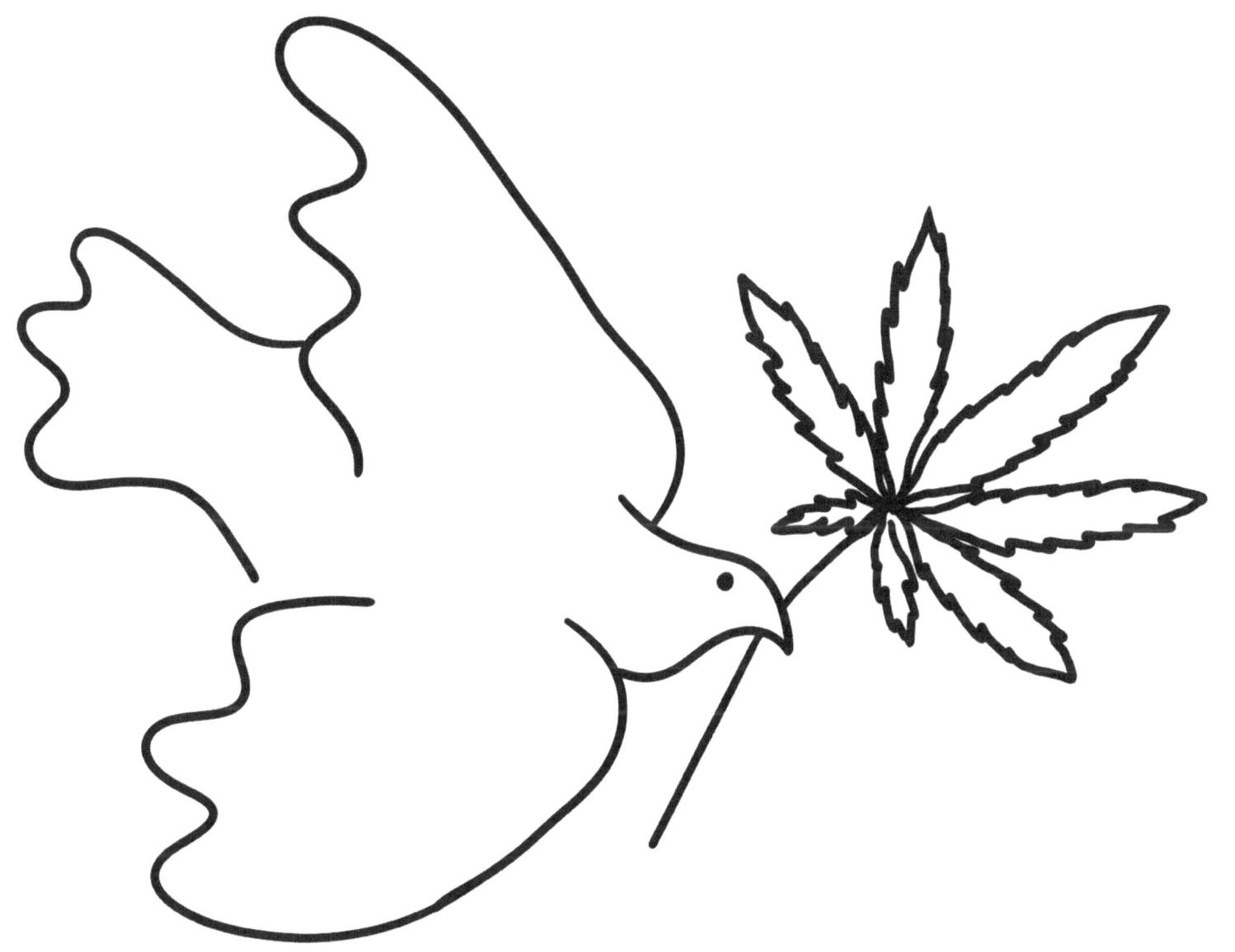

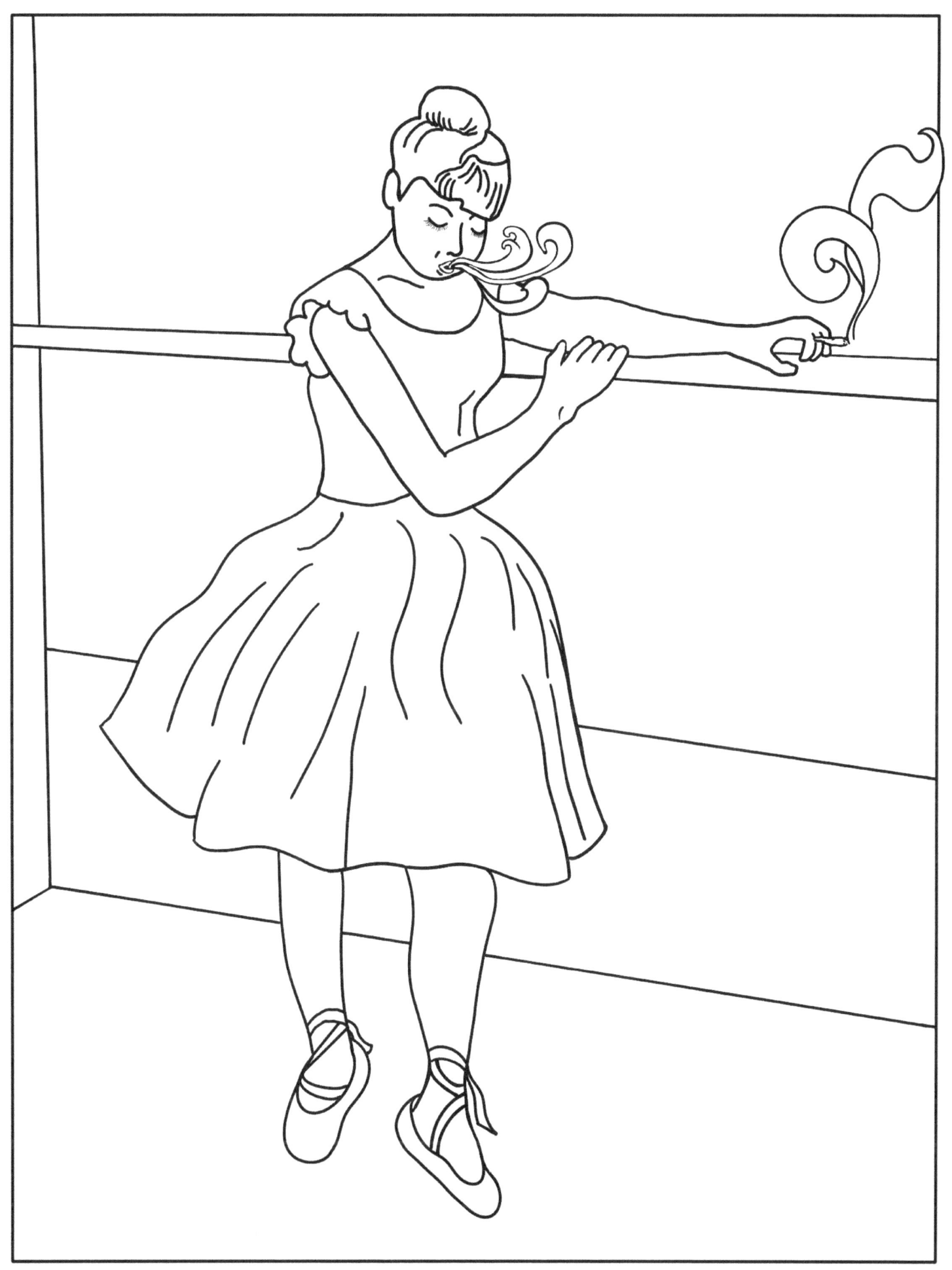

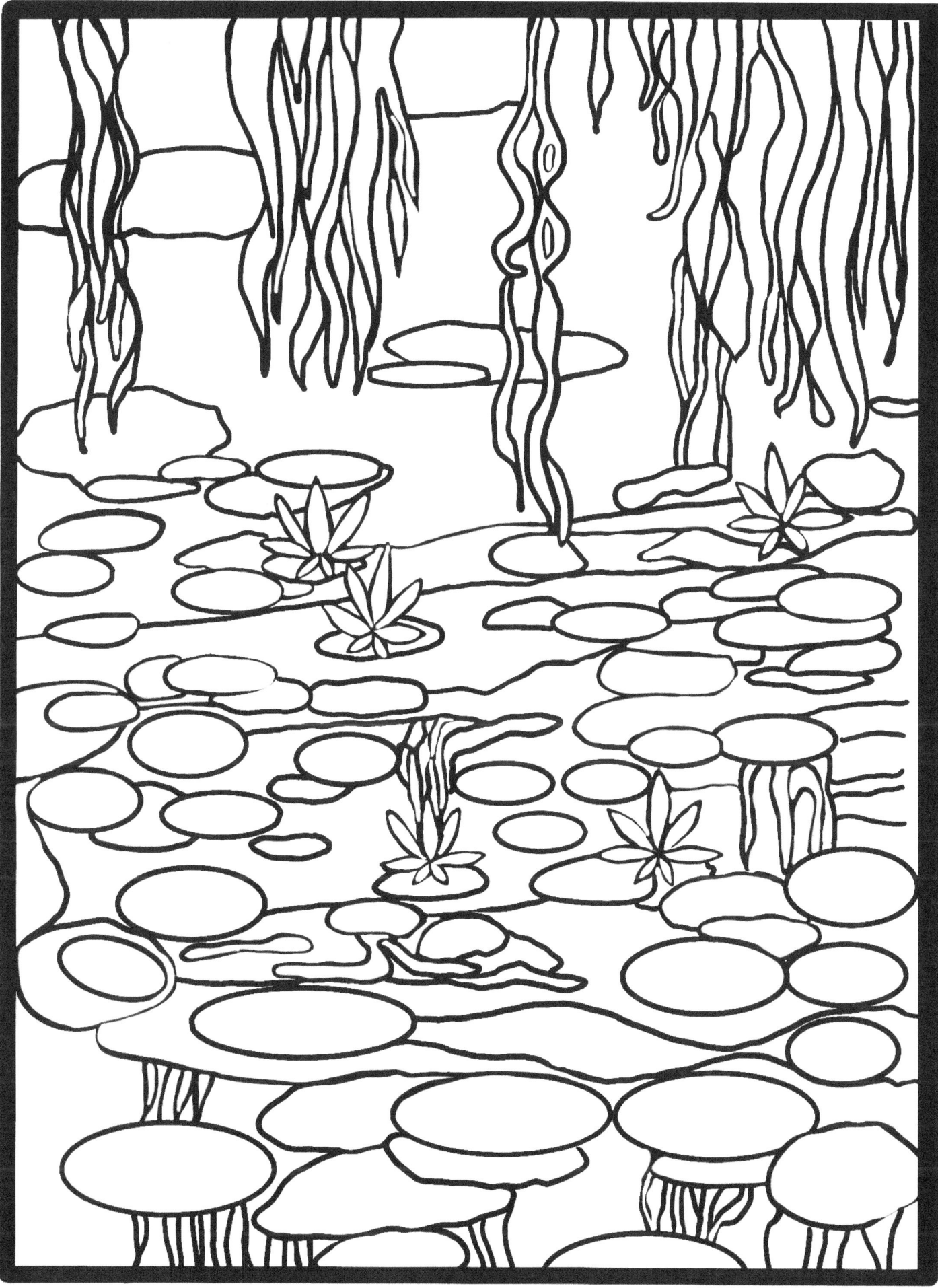

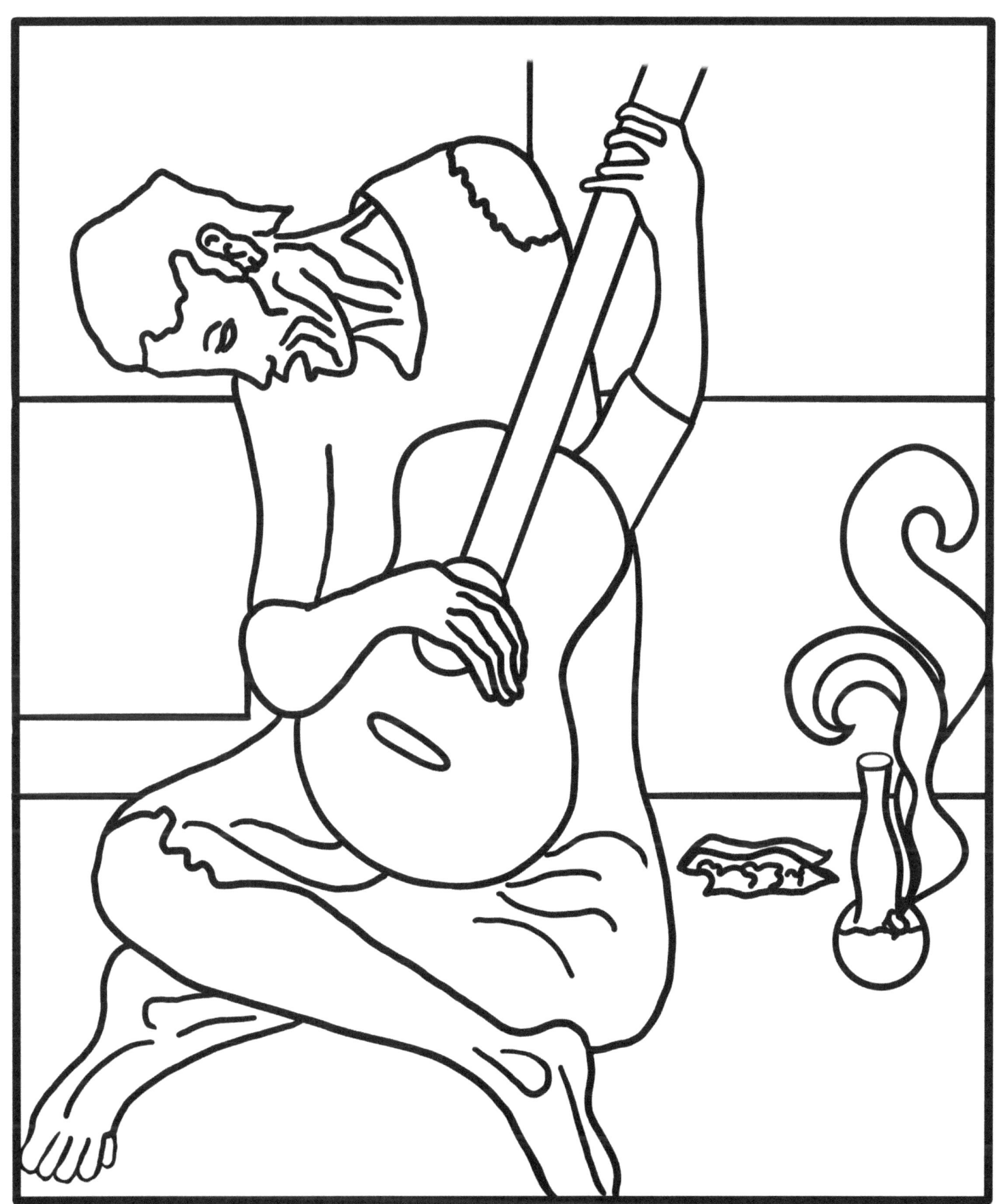

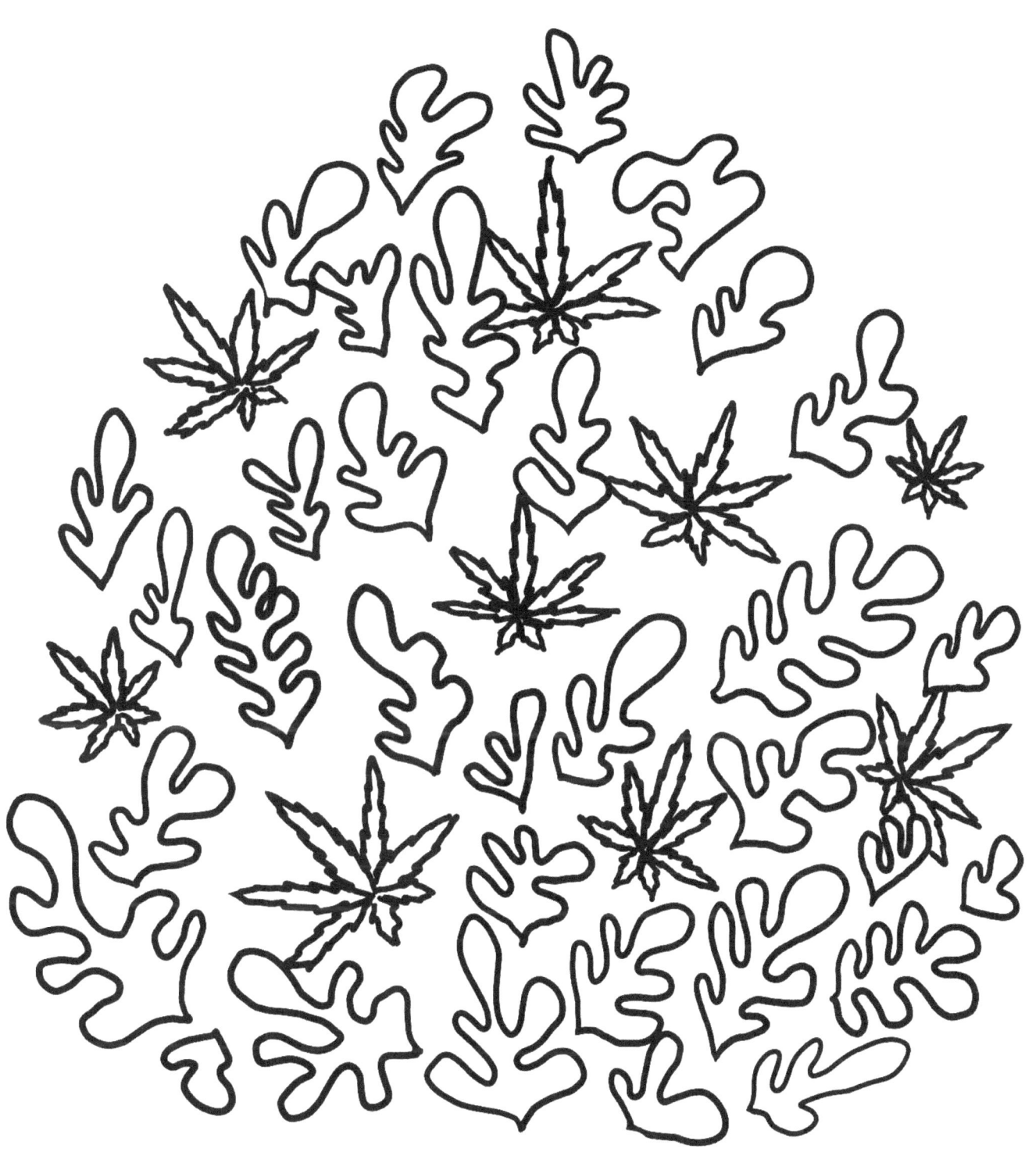

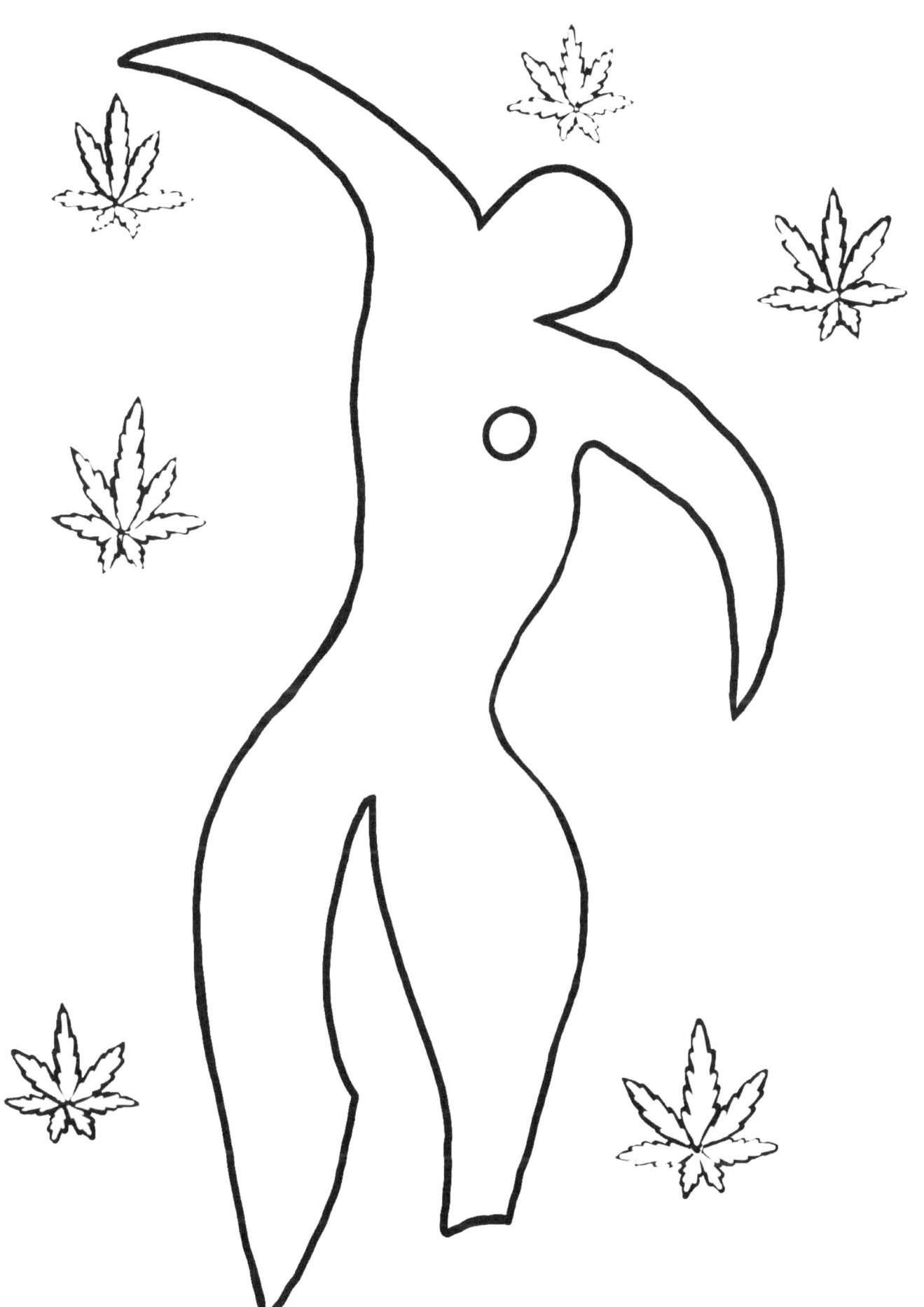

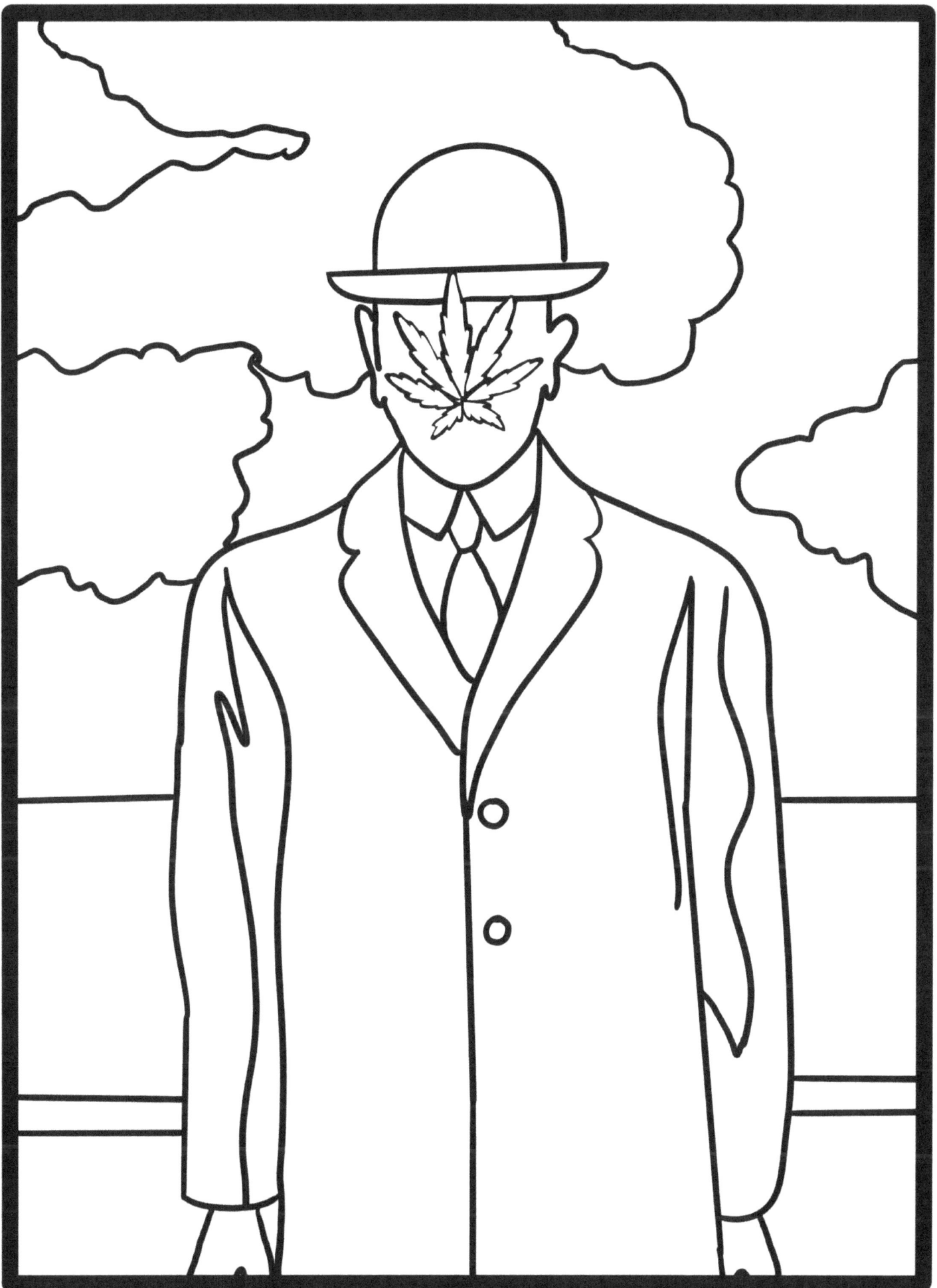

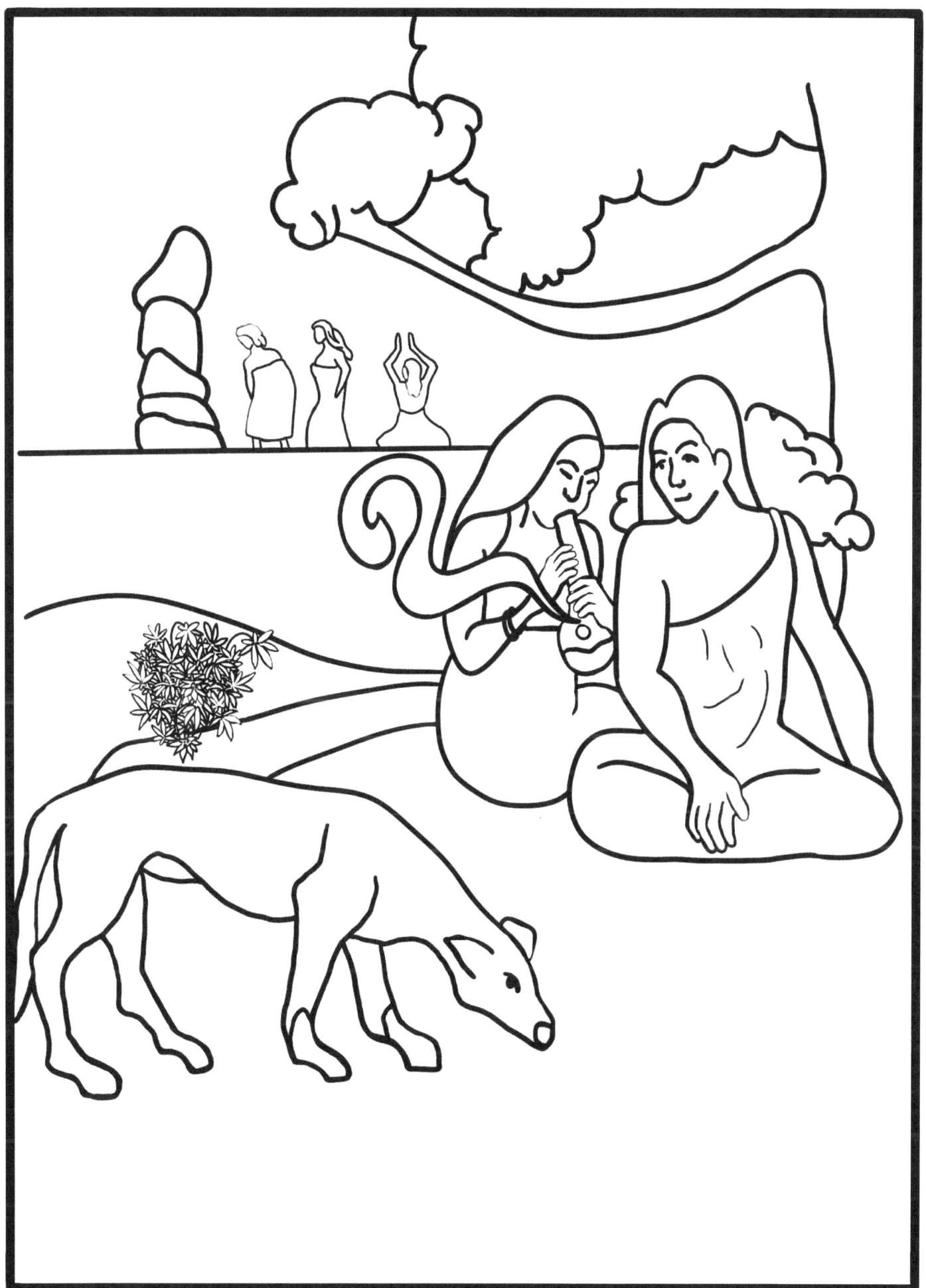

www.ingramcontent.com/pod-product-compliance
Lightning Source LLC
Chambersburg PA
CBHW080839220526
45467CB00008B/2335